Your Guide to
Retirement

Ro Lyon

BOOKS

© 2003 Age Concern England
Published by Age Concern England
1268 London Road
London SW16 4ER

First published 1993 as The Retirement Handbook
Second edition 1997
Revised 2000
Reprinted 2001
First published 2003 under the new title Your Guide to Retirement

Editor Marion Peat
Production Vinnette Marshall
Design and Typesetting GreenGate Publishing Services, Tonbridge, Kent
Printed in Great Britain by Bell & Bain Ltd, Glasgow

A catalogue record for this book is available from the British Library

ISBN 0-86242-350-3

Bulk orders

Age Concern England is pleased to offer customised editions of all its titles to UK companies, institutions or other organisations wishing to make a bulk purchase. For further information, please contact the Publishing Department at the address on this page. Tel: 020 8765 7200. Fax: 020 8765 7211. Email: books@ace.org.uk

Contents

Introduction v

Managing money I

Pensions and benefits 2

Your tax position 28

Your savings and investments 35

Making a will 45

Managing another person's money 49

Making the most of your time 53

Learning opportunities 54

Community involvement 59

Earning money in retirement 64

Travel 74

Going on holiday 81

Your home 91

Moving house 92

Home security 107

Repairs and improvements 110

Raising income or capital from your home 118

Staying healthy 123

Looking after your body 124

Health problems 137

Help with health costs 147

Relationships 149

Sex in later life 150

Bereavement 157

Caring for someone 166

Further information 175

Useful addresses 176

About Age Concern 197

Publications from Age Concern Books 198

Index 205

Introduction

Some people look forward eagerly to retirement, some dread it; most people probably fall somewhere between these two extremes. Whatever your attitude, however positive your feelings, retirement is a time of adjustment – and adjustment is not always easy.

Retirement may mean that you have more control over your life than ever before: the 50 or so hours that were taken up by work and travelling to work are now yours to spend as you like. The fact that you are working can sometimes provide convenient excuses:

- I have always wanted to take up painting but I never have time.
- I'm unfit but am always too busy and tired to do anything about it.
- I know the house needs a lot doing to it, but I seem to spend the whole weekend just catching up.

Leaving work strips away all these excuses at once. Whereas an extra couple of hours a day free might have seemed like an unqualified bonus, having the whole week free to spend as you choose may seem positively daunting.

Retirement can cause stress in people's relationships. One partner may retire and want to embark on all sorts of joint activities, while the other is still working and too busy to take on anything extra. Couples who have been married 30 or 40 years may find their relationship under strain if they are suddenly thrown together for 24 hours a day. You may find yourselves having to work out afresh how you're going to live together, just as you did when you were first married.

People who live alone may worry about missing the day-to-day companionship provided by going to work. People who are disabled or in poor health may feel anxious about how they will cope as they get older and frustrated by being unable to do all the things they could hope to do.

To help ease the transition, many employers provide retirement courses for their employees. In addition to providing practical information and suggestions, these can give people a chance to talk about their hopes and expectations, their fears and anxieties. Some courses include people's partners.

The aim of this book

This book aims to provide people who are about to retire or have just retired with suggestions and practical information that will be useful for the years ahead.

Chapter 1 looks at the various aspects of managing money, as having an adequate income is essential whatever your plans for the future. Chapter 2 looks at ways of using your time, including educational opportunities, doing voluntary work, earning money, and travel. Chapter 3 discusses the issues related to your home, including whether or not to move house and repairs and maintenance.

Staying as healthy as possible is vital if you are to get the most out of retirement. Chapter 4 looks at positive steps you can take to maintain – or even improve – your health. It also looks at certain health problems which may affect older people and at the help that is available with health costs. Chapter 5 considers the ways in which retirement can affect relationships, focusing on sexual relationships, coping with bereavement and caring for someone.

The aim is to outline the main points for each topic and then to point you in the right direction to obtain more information if you need it. The final chapter of the book gives contact details for sources of further help. The book is based on information available in November 2002. There may have been later changes to payment rates in particular, so make sure you have further up-to-date information before taking action.

But the aim of this book is not simply to provide information. It aims also to encourage – to encourage you to make the most of the opportunities offered by retirement, to regard retirement in a positive light, to see it not as the closing of one door but as the opening of many.

Managing money

'How well off am I going to be?' is a question that is likely to concern anyone on the verge of retirement. Whatever your plans, they are likely to depend to some extent on the state of your finances.

When considering your financial position, there are certain questions it is worth asking yourself: Are you receiving all the pensions and benefits you are entitled to? Are you paying more tax than you should? Could your savings be better invested?

This chapter looks at all these issues. It also looks at making a will and managing another person's money.

- Pensions and benefits
- Your tax position
- Your savings and investments
- Making a will
- Managing another person's money

Pensions and benefits

Factfile

- There are over 10.7 million people of pensionable age in the UK (60 or over for women, 65 or over for men).

- This comprises roughly 18 per cent of the population.

- In 2000 there were 6,915,000 women and 3,875,000 men of pensionable age.

Most people receive a State Retirement Pension when they retire. If you have an occupational pension, this may well be a significant source of income once you leave work. People who are self-employed, and employees who did not belong to a company scheme, may have a personal pension. Many people will have income from a number of different pensions. This section looks at the different types of pension and at the various State benefits that are available to people with low incomes and to people with disabilities and their carers.

The State Retirement Pension

To qualify for the State Retirement Pension you must have:

- reached State Pension age (60 for women, 65 for men); and
- fulfilled the National Insurance (NI) contributions (described below).

Your Retirement Pension may consist of a Basic Pension, an Additional Pension and a Graduated Pension. People over 80 who have not paid enough contributions for a Basic Pension may receive a non-contributory pension (£45.20 a week in 2002–2003 and due to be £46.35 in 2003–2004). All elements of the Retirement Pension are taxable.

Parliament has passed legislation to equalise the State Pension age at 65 for both men and women. This is to be phased in over ten years, starting in 2010. No one born before 5 April 1950 will be affected by the change.

Pensions and other benefits are normally updated in April every year. The new rates are generally announced the preceding autumn.

> ## Factfile
>
> ■ In 2000–2001 single pensioners received, on average, £160 net income per week.
>
> ■ Pensioner couples received £301 per week on average during the same period.
>
> ■ The Basic Pension from April 2002 to April 2003 is £75.50 for a single pensioner, or £120.70 for a couple (claiming on the husband's contributions) per week. In 2003–2004 the figures will be £77.45 and £123.80.

The Basic Pension

The Basic Pension is paid at the same rate to everyone who has fulfilled the contribution conditions – £75.50 a week for a single person in 2002–2003 (£77.45 in 2003–2004) and £45.20 (£46.35 in 2003–2004) for a wife on the basis of her husband's contributions, with an extra 25p for people over 80.

Increases for dependants If you are a married man and your wife is under 60 when you draw your pension, you may be able to claim an increase for her as a dependant (up to £46.35 a week in 2002–2003). If your wife receives certain other State benefits or earns more than a set amount (including any occupational or personal pension), you may not be able to receive this.

If you are a married woman you may be able to claim a similar dependant's increase for your husband, provided you were claiming an increase for him with Incapacity Benefit (see pages 24–25) immediately before you started drawing your pension.

The contribution conditions You will get the full Basic Pension if you have paid, or been credited with, NI contributions for most of your 'working life'.

Working life This is the number of tax years during which you are expected to pay, or be credited with, NI contributions. It normally starts in the tax year when you were 16 and ends with the last full tax year before you are 60 (women) or 65 (men).

Qualifying year This is a tax year in which you have paid, or been credited with, enough contributions to go towards a pension. To be entitled to a full pension, about nine out of every ten years of your working life have to be 'qualifying years'. If you have not got enough qualifying years to qualify for a full pension, you may receive a reduced pension or none at all.

Pension forecast You can find out whether you have paid enough contributions to get a full pension by completing form BR 19, which you can get from your local social security office. Alternatively, you can get an estimate by phoning the Pension Service on 0191 218 7585 (weekdays). Your contribution record may be better than you expect because you have received credits or Home Responsibilities Protection.

Credits may be given if you are under pension age and you are registered for Jobseeker's Allowance; or you are unable to work because you are sick or disabled; or you receive Invalid Care Allowance. Men aged 60–64 who are not paying contributions normally receive credits automatically.

Home Responsibilities Protection (HRP) HRP protects the contribution record of people who cannot work regularly because they have to stay at home to look after children or a sick or disabled person. HRP makes it easier for you to qualify for a full Basic Pension: each year of 'home responsibility' will be taken away from the number of qualifying years you need to get a full pension – although it cannot be used to reduce the number of qualifying years below 20.

In some circumstances you receive HRP automatically, but sometimes you need to claim it – check the position with your local social security office. From April 2002 you have to claim by the end of the third year following the year for which you are claiming. HRP does not apply to years before 1978.

Late or voluntary contributions You may be able to pay these if there are gaps in your contribution record.

For more information, see Inland Revenue leaflets CA 08 (on voluntary contributions) and CA 07 (late contributions). Details of how to obtain Inland Revenue leaflets are given on page 178.

Normally you need to have satisfied the contribution conditions in your own right, but there are the following exceptions:

Married women of 60 or over who have not paid enough contributions for a pension in their own right can draw the married woman's pension (£45.20 a week in 2002–2003; £46.35 in 2003–2004) when their husband draws his pension, depending on his contribution record. Any years for which you paid married woman's reduced-rate contributions will not count towards a pension in your own right.

Separated women who do not qualify for a pension in their own right may be able to claim a married woman's pension on their husband's contributions in the same way.

Divorced people who do not remarry before pension age, and who do not qualify for a full pension in their own right, may be able to substitute their former spouse's contribution record for their own, either just for the period of the marriage or from the start of their working life up until the divorce, in order to draw a full Basic Pension. You are not entitled to your former spouse's Graduated or Additional Pension, although since December 2000 it has been possible under the 'pension sharing' rules to divide the Additional Pension as part of a divorce settlement.

Widows who do not remarry before State Pension age can draw a Basic Pension on their own and/or their husband's contributions. The amount you receive will depend upon your, and your late husband's, contribution record and the age at which you were widowed. You may also receive Additional and/or Graduated Pension based on your husband's contributions (see pages 6 and 7). Once you have reached State Pension age and are drawing a State Pension, widows (or widowers) can remarry without losing the pension based on their previous spouse's contributions.

Widowers may be entitled to a Basic Pension on their wife's contributions, provided they were both over State Pension age when she died. You may also inherit some of your wife's Additional Pension and/or Graduated pension. If you were widowed before age 65, once you reach pension age you may be able to substitute your late wife's contribution record for your own in order to increase your Basic Pension up to the maximum of £75.50 a week.

Additional Pension

If you have worked and paid contributions since April 1978, you may receive some Additional Pension on top of any Basic Pension you receive. This is taxable and based on earnings. You may qualify for an Additional Pension even if you do not have the minimum number of qualifying years for a Basic Pension.

From 1978 to April 2002, Additional Pension was built up under the State Earnings-Related Pension Scheme (SERPS), but from April 2002 the State Second Pension (S2P) has replaced SERPS (see below).

The Additional Pension is related to weekly earnings between certain levels known as the 'lower and upper earnings limits'. Earnings from past years are revalued in line with increases in average earnings. The amount of Additional Pension paid is being tapered down between 1999 and 2009 from 25 per cent to 20 per cent of earnings between the specified levels. However, under S2P the amount of Additional Pension that you earn is calculated in a different way.

For any years during which you belong to a 'contracted out' occupational pension scheme or an approved personal pension scheme, you will not be part of SERPS/S2P, as explained on page 12. The Additional Pension does not apply to self-employed people.

When a widow starts to receive her Retirement Pension at 60, or if she is already receiving her pension at the time she is widowed, she can inherit all or some of her husband's Additional Pension (adjusted for periods when he was contracted out of SERPS/S2P). As a widow any amount you are entitled to is added to any Additional Pension on your own contributions up to the maximum amount a single person could receive. The amount you can inherit depends on when your husband dies and when he reaches, or was due to reach, State Pension age. Similar rules apply to a widower if both he and his wife are over pension age when she dies.

For information about how Additional Pension is calculated, see social security guide NP 46. For information about inheritance of SERPS, see leaflet SERPS L1. Details of how to obtain social security leaflets are given on page 177.

State Second Pension (S2P)

The State Second Pension replaced SERPS for contributions made from April 2002. Like SERPS it is earnings-related but it provides extra pension to certain carers, disabled people and low-paid workers.

If you have already reached pension age, you will not be affected. If you reach pension age after April 2002, you may have an Additional Pension built up partly under SERPS and partly under S2P. SERPS benefits already built up have been safeguarded.

Graduated Pension

The Graduated Pension scheme existed from April 1961 to April 1975 and was based on graduated contributions paid from earnings. The weekly rate that women receive in 2002–2003 is 9.21p for every £9 of contributions paid, while men receive 9.21p for every £7.50 paid. (In 2003–2004 it will be 9.37p for every £9 for women and 9.37p for every £7.50 for men.) You can receive Graduated Pension even if you do not qualify for a Basic Pension.

A widow can inherit half of her late husband's Graduated Pension, as can a widower (provided that they were both over pension age when she died).

Claiming your pension

About four months before you reach State Pension age (60 for women, 65 for men) you should be sent a claim pack. If you do not receive one, contact the Pension Service or ring 0845 300 1084. A married woman claiming a pension on her husband's contributions will need to make a separate claim. Your pension can be backdated for up to three months if you make a late claim.

You can currently choose to have your pension paid by weekly order book which you cash at a post office or directly into a bank, building society, or post office account. However, the Government is changing the system so that by 2005 nearly everyone will have payment directly into an account. If you receive a letter inviting you to change, contact a local advice agency.

If you think you have been awarded the wrong amount of pension, you can either ask to have the decision revised or you can appeal against it.

Going abroad or living there

If you receive your pension by weekly order book and are going abroad for less than three months, you can cash your pension orders when you come home. If you are going abroad for longer, tell your social security office well in advance. If you do not receive your pension by weekly order book, you do not have to tell your local office unless you are staying abroad for more than six months. You can, if you wish, arrange to receive your pension in the country where you are staying. If you remain abroad, the annual pension increase will be paid only if you are living in a EU country or in a country with which the UK has special arrangements.

For more information contact your social security office or the Pension Service Overseas Branch at the address on page 178.

If you carry on working after pension age

Your State Pension will not be affected by the amount you earn or the number of hours you work (although money earned will be subject to Income Tax). However, if you draw an increase for a dependent husband or wife, this may be affected by their earnings, as explained on page 3.

Deferring your pension

You can choose to defer (postpone) drawing your pension for up to five years in order to earn extra pension. Even if you start drawing your pension, you can change your mind and defer it instead – but you can only do this once.

If you defer your pension, it is increased by about 7.5 per cent for each full year that you do not draw it – or by 37.5 per cent over the full five years which would bring the Basic Pension up to about £106 a week (2003 figure). Your Additional and Graduated Pensions are increased in the same way.

Extra pension for married women If you are aged 60–64 and entitled to a pension on your husband's contributions, you can defer this to gain an increase. If your husband defers his pension, you will not be able to draw yours at pensionable age until he draws his. Then you will both receive increases. If, while your husband is deferring his pension, you draw another benefit such as Additional Pension or Graduated Pension, your pension on your husband's contributions will not be increased. It may therefore be better not to draw a small Additional or Graduated Pension if your husband is deferring his pension.

For more information on deferring your pension, see Age Concern Factsheet 19 *The State Pension*. Details of how to obtain Age Concern factsheets are given on page 204.

If you stop working before pension age

If you retire early, make sure that you qualify for a full Retirement Pension when you reach pension age – check your contribution record with your local social security office. You receive credits automatically if you are receiving a benefit such as Incapacity Benefit or Jobseeker's Allowance (JSA), or if you are a man aged 60–64, unless you are abroad for more than half the year. If you are under 60 and seeking work it may be worth registering for JSA even if you are not entitled to benefit, because you will then receive credits. If you are not entitled to credits, you may want to consider paying voluntary contributions.

Although you cannot draw a State Retirement Pension before pension age, there are other benefits you may be able to claim:

Jobseeker's Allowance is a taxable benefit for people who are unemployed and who are 'actively seeking' full-time work and have a current 'Jobseeker's Agreement'. JSA stops at the age of 60 for women and 65 for men. There are two elements: contribution-based JSA, which is based on your NI contribution record, and income-based JSA, which is means-tested.

Contribution-based JSA can be paid for up to 26 weeks (£53.95 a week in 2002–2003; £54.65 in 2003–2004). There are no additions for dependants. This will be reduced if you have an occupational or personal pension of over £50 a week.

Income-based JSA can be paid in addition to contribution-based JSA or on its own after 26 weeks, depending on your income and savings. The rules for calculating benefit are similar to those for Income Support, described on pages 18–19.

Incapacity Benefit Depending on your NI contribution record, you may be entitled to this benefit, which is described on pages 24–25.

Income Support (also known for people aged 60 and over as the Minimum Income Guarantee) Depending on your income and savings, you may be entitled to Income Support, as described on pages 18–20 or, from October 2003, Pension Credit, described on page 20.

Housing Benefit and/or Council Tax Benefit You may be entitled to these benefits, depending on your income and savings (see pages 21–22). You may qualify for some benefit even if you do not qualify for Income Support or income-based JSA.

Increasing your State Pension

If you have had an interrupted career, check what credits you are entitled to – including HRP, which you may have to claim (see page 4). If there are gaps in your contribution record, you may be able to pay voluntary contributions. You can do this only for gaps within the last six years. Ask for a pension forecast first, however (see page 4): there is no point in paying extra contributions if you have already met the contribution requirements for a full Basic Pension.

The only other way to increase your State Basic Pension is to defer drawing your pension, as explained above. It is wise to take advice before doing this: it may be better to draw the pension and invest it.

Age Concern Books' annual publication *Your Rights* (see page 198) gives full details of the State Pension and other State benefits available to older people.

Occupational pensions

Factfile

■ In 2000–2001 60 per cent of pensioners received occupational pensions. The median pension received was £65 per week.

Occupational pensions are also known as 'company pensions' and are run by employers. There are two main types:

Earnings-related schemes (also called 'final salary' or 'salary related'), which give a pension based on a proportion of final earnings – typically either ⅟₆₀th or ⅟₈₀th of your final salary for each year worked. Some will offer a cash lump sum as well. Altogether benefits cannot exceed two thirds of your final pay. Often only part of your pay is pensionable – check in your scheme booklet. How well your pension keeps up with inflation will depend on whether or not it is index-linked. Such schemes are mainly found in the public sector or from some bigger companies. They can also be called 'defined benefit' schemes because it is the amount of pension which is guaranteed, not the contributions you pay.

Money-purchase schemes, which give a pension based on the value of the pension fund you have built up. The contributions you and your employer pay are invested, and the proceeds of the fund are used to buy an annuity (a lifetime pension). The amount of the annuity will depend on how well the investments have done, how long you have been paying into the pension fund, your age and sex, the annuity rates at the time you draw your pension and which type of annuity you purchase. These schemes can also be called 'defined contribution' schemes because it is the amount you pay in which is fixed, not the pension you get at the end.

Contracted in or out?

Occupational pension schemes can be 'contracted in' or 'contracted out' of the State Second Pension (S2P), and previously the State Earnings-Related Pension Scheme (SERPS). If you are a member of a contracted-in scheme, you will receive SERPS/S2P as well as your occupational pension. If you are a member of a contracted-out scheme, you will have been paying lower National Insurance contributions and you will receive an occupational pension instead of the SERPS/S2P.

To be allowed to contract out of S2P (and previously SERPS), the scheme must meet some minimum standards, but these have changed over time. Until April 1997, members of a contracted-out salary-related scheme had to receive a minimum amount called the Guaranteed Minimum Pension (GMP): this is roughly the same as you would have received if you had stayed in SERPS. However, for any pension that built up after April 1997, the scheme does not have to provide a specific GMP; instead schemes have to meet certain conditions in order to be contracted out of SERPS/S2P.

If you belong to a contracted-out money-purchase scheme you will have Protected Rights, which may be more or less than the Additional Pension you would have received. For this sort of scheme (but not a salary-related one) contracting out is disadvantageous for older people and those with low earnings. If you think this might apply to you, check with the pension administrator or the scheme's financial adviser.

The lump sum

With both types of scheme you have the option of taking a certain amount as a lump sum and getting a lower pension. Your pension will be treated as taxable earnings, but the lump sum is tax-free. Most people take the maximum lump sum, but if you belong to a good index-linked scheme, it may be better to take a higher pension rather than the lump sum. The rate at which you exchange the pension for cash can also vary considerably.

Pensions and divorce

In the past, it was not possible to divide an occupational pension between a husband and wife who got divorced. For divorces where the petition was issued after 1 December 2000, however, 'pension sharing' is now available. This means that an occupational, stakeholder, or personal pension can be divided at the time of divorce, and the ex-spouse can generally then transfer it elsewhere. Even if you were divorced before that date, it may be possible to petition the court – the rules are complex, so seek legal advice.

Collecting from former pension schemes

If you have changed jobs in the past, you may have pensions preserved or 'frozen' in former employers' schemes, which you will have to claim. The Pensions Schemes Registry (at the address on page 178) can give former employers' addresses so that you can contact them yourself.

If you have any problems with pensions that you cannot sort out with the pension provider, contact the Pensions Advisory Service (OPAS) at the address on page 178.

Increasing your occupational pension

The most you can pay into your company scheme is 15 per cent of your gross pay. Most company schemes take far less than that and you can make up the difference by paying into Additional Voluntary Contributions (AVCs). AVCs are designed to top up your company pension. They are paid into a separate money purchase scheme either through your employer or, if you choose, separately from your employer, in which case they are called Free-standing Additional Voluntary Contributions (FSAVCs). Since April 2001, if you earn £30,000 or less, you can also pay up to £2,808 into a stakeholder pension on top of any occupational pension you may have, and the Chancellor will top this up by £792 to make a gross contribution to your pension fund of £3,600.

The older you are, the less time you have to contribute to a pension fund and for your contribution to grow in value. So if you are paying in extra over only a short period, you will need to put in the maximum the Inland Revenue allows.

For more information, see the Financial Services Authority's *Guide to Topping Up your Occupational Pension*, which is available from the FSA at the address on page 177.

Personal pensions

You can buy a personal pension at any age until your 75th birthday, whether you have earnings or not, although if you belong to an occupational scheme there are special rules about buying a personal pension in addition. You can draw your pension any time between the ages of 50 and 75.

Personal pensions come in three sorts, depending on when you started contributing to them:

- Before June 1988 – retirement annuity contracts or Section 226 pensions.
- From 1 June 1988 – personal pension plans.
- From 6 April 2001 – stakeholder pensions – a special sort of personal pension.

Personal pensions are money-purchase schemes in that your pension is based on a pension fund built up over the years. You can take up to 25 per cent of the fund as a tax-free lump sum and must use the rest to buy an annuity (a lifetime pension).

Personal pensions are provided by financial institutions, such as banks, building societies and insurance companies. There are two types – those that are 'appropriate' (for contracting out of SERPS/S2P) and those that are not.

When stakeholder pensions were introduced in April 2001, the rules about contributions were relaxed and now apply to personal pensions as well. All contributions to a personal pension are now paid net of basic-rate tax relief. In the past you paid in £100 out of your income before tax (and payments into a retirement annuity contract are still paid in this way). But with personal pensions you now pay in £78 and the Chancellor pays in the other £22. If you are a higher-rate taxpayer you can then recover £18 tax when you fill in your self-assessment form. So your net contribution for £100 in your pension is just £60.

If you are working and you are not paying into an occupational pension scheme, or if you are self-employed, the amount that can be paid into a personal pension depends on your age. If you are aged 56 to 60, you can pay in 35 per cent of your gross pay (or £91,800 if that is lower) or 40 per cent if you are 61 or over.

There are various types of personal pension:

Deposit-based policies are similar to ordinary savings accounts. They make safe havens for people nearing retirement who do not want to take any risk with the fund they have already built up, but the returns may well be lower than for other types of policy.

With-profits policies offer some guaranteed return. Bonuses which cannot be taken away are added during the lifetime of the plan, and there will usually also be a variable 'terminal' bonus at the end.

Unit-linked policies – with this type, your contributions are invested in unit trusts (see page 42) and the value of the fund is directly related to the market performance of the units that are purchased.

People approaching retirement are normally advised to gradually shift their pension funds out of share-based investments and into less volatile investments. If you have not yet retired, ask for advice on how and when to switch.

Buying an annuity

You must use your pension fund (minus the lump sum) to buy an annuity. Only insurance companies can provide annuities. How much you get will depend on your age, sex and health, the insurance company chosen, and interest rates at the time of purchase. An annuity is essentially insurance against living too long and so the price you have to pay for each £1 of income goes down as you get older. Insurance companies invest the annuity money in very safe lending to the Government, but this means that when interest rates fall (because inflation is low) the price you must pay for an annuity rises.

You do not have to buy the annuity from your pension provider. You have an 'open market option' (OMO), which your pension provider must tell you about (on at least two occasions in the four months before you retire) and which allows you to choose any insurance company where the annuity rates may be better. You should also receive a copy of the Financial Services Authority's (FSA's) factsheet *Your pension: it's time to choose*. Rates vary considerably, so you could improve your pension by as much as 35 per cent by shopping around. However, there may also be a fee or commission to pay to your adviser, so taking up the OMO may not be worthwhile if you have only a small fund.

You can draw income directly from the fund, up until the year you are 75, rather than taking an annuity. This is called 'income drawdown' but is usually only worthwhile if you have a very large fund, as the charges for managing the investment are high.

There is a variety of annuities available, including:

- **Flat-rate annuities** where the income you receive remains fixed from the outset.
- **Escalating annuities** where the income increases annually to help off-set inflation. But you will receive a lower starting income than with a flat-rate annuity. You can buy one linked to the Retail Price Index or one that increases annually at a fixed percentage rate.
- **Dependants' benefits** which provide income after your death for a spouse or dependant children.
- **Guaranteed period annuities** where the income is guaranteed for a fixed period: if you die before that time, the income is paid into your estate.
- **Unit-linked annuities** where the income is linked to the investment returns achieved by the insurance companies, and so can vary considerably.

An independent financial adviser (see page 36) should be able to find the best value for you at the time, but you will get better advice if you have worked out your requirements already. There are choices to be made before you buy, such as whether you want: a high starting level that is fixed or a lower one that increases each year; a guarantee that the pension will be paid for a minimum period; a pension that will continue until your spouse's death; and/or payments monthly or quarterly. From Spring

2003 the FSA website (www.fsa.gov.uk) will include comparative tables providing information to help consumers choose an annuity.

Increasing a personal pension

Personal pensions have generous contribution limits, increasing with age.

'Carry-back facilities' enable you to ask for a contribution paid in the current year to be treated as if it was paid in the previous year – which is helpful if your income was much higher that year.

If you have already reached State Pension age, but are continuing to earn or have other sources of income, you can continue paying into a personal pension until you are 75. You can put in 40 per cent of your earnings and receive tax relief. However, as the money will only be in the fund for a short time, make sure that the pension contract does not penalise short-stayers.

Single-premium personal pensions enable you to pay a single contribution, on which you get full tax relief, and draw the pension and tax-free lump sum immediately, even if you are not yet retiring (provided you are aged 50 or over). Paying single premiums also avoids your having to commit yourself to making regular payments.

For more details about all types of pension, see Age Concern Books' annual publication *The Pensions Handbook* (see page 198).

Benefits for people with low incomes

There are certain State benefits that are available to people whose income and savings are below a certain level. Income Support (Minimum Income Guarantee) and the forthcoming Pension Credit, Housing Benefit and Council Tax Benefit all help with regular living expenses, while the Social Fund provides lump-sum payments for exceptional expenses. Many older people will be entitled to extra money as a result of the introduction of the Pension Credit in October 2003. In addition, people with low incomes may be able to get financial help towards such expenses as house repairs and dental care.

If, for example, you leave work before you reach State Pension age and only have a small occupational pension, it may be worth checking whether you are eligible for any of these benefits. Many older people are entitled to benefits but do not make a claim, so make sure that you are not missing out on income that is due to you.

Factfile

- In 2000–2001, 69 per cent of pensioner households depended on State benefits for at least 50 per cent of their income.

- In February 2002, 1,737,000 people aged 60 or over (single people and couples) were receiving Income Support (Minimum Income Guarantee) because of their low income.

- It is estimated that, in 1999–2000, between 22 per cent and 36 per cent of pensioners who were entitled to Income Support did not claim it.

Income Support

For people aged 60 or over, Income Support is known as the Minimum Income Guarantee or MIG. Income Support tops up your income to a weekly level set by the Government. You do not need to have paid NI contributions to qualify. You may receive Income Support if:

- You are aged 60 or over or you are under 60 but do not need to register for Jobseeker's Allowance (JSA), for example because you are ill or because you are a carer. Unemployed people receive income-based JSA instead.
- Your savings are £12,000 or less if you are aged 60 or over (£16,000 if you live in a care home or £8,000 if you are aged under 60).
- You have a low income.
- You do not work 16 hours a week or more and your partner, if you have one, does not work 24 hours a week or more.
- You are 'habitually resident' in the UK.

To work out whether you qualify, you need to:

1 **Add up the value of your savings** If your savings (and capital) are more than £12,000 (£16,000 for people in a care home or £8,000 for people aged under 60), you will not be eligible. For a couple savings are added together, but the limit is the same. (You will count as a couple if you are married or you live with someone of the opposite sex as though you were married.) If you have savings between £6,000 and £12,000 (£3,000 and £8,000 for people aged under 60), income of £1 per week for every £250 (or part of £250) over £6,000 (or £3,000) will be taken into account when your benefit is worked out. This is known as 'tariff income'. Some savings will be ignored, including the value of your home.

2 **Add up your income** including earnings, State benefits, occupational, personal and stakeholder pensions, and any tariff income on savings between £6,000 and £12,000 (£3,000 and £8,000 if you are under 60). Certain income will be ignored, including Housing Benefit and Council Tax Benefit and actual interest on savings. For a couple, the income of both partners is added together.

3 **Work out your applicable amount** This is the weekly amount intended to meet your everyday living needs. It is worked out by adding together the personal allowance (£53.95 for a single person, £84.65 for a couple, in 2002–2003, and due to be £54.65 and £85.75 in 2003–2004) and any premiums that apply to you. Premiums are extra amounts awarded to people over 60, disabled people and carers who are entitled to Invalid Care Allowance (see page 27).

4 **Compare your income with your applicable amount** If your income is less than your applicable amount, you will qualify for Income Support (depending on your savings). If your income is more, you will not get Income Support but you may still get Housing Benefit or Council Tax Benefit. To understand what housing costs you might be entitled to, you may need to get further information from your local Age Concern or an advice agency.

To claim Income Support you should obtain a claim form from your local social security office. The local CAB or advice agency will also be able to help you fill in the form.

For more information about how your savings and income affect your entitlement to income-related benefits, see Age Concern Factsheet 16 *Income-related benefits: income and capital.* See also Factsheet 25 *Income Support (Minimum Income Guarantee) and the Social Fund.*

Pension Credit

In October 2003 a new Pension Credit will replace Income Support and provide extra cash to people who have saved. It will have two parts – the guarantee credit and the savings credit. The 'guarantee credit' will replace Income Support for people aged 60 or over. Like Income Support, the guarantee credit will top up someone's income to a set amount, which will be in line with their current Income Support applicable amount.

The savings credit will be for people aged 65 and over and will provide extra cash to those who have income of more than the level of the Basic State Pension and less than certain levels – for most people around £139 a week (£204 for a couple). It will therefore help people on modest incomes who have income in addition to the Basic State Pension, such as occupational pensions, the State Additional Pension or income from savings.

As with Income Support, the first £6,000 of savings will be ignored but the upper limit will be removed. Any savings of over £6,000 will be counted as £1 a week assumed income for every £500 (or part of £500) over £6,000 (for Income Support it is £1 for every £250). The new system of assumed income will also apply to Housing and Council Tax Benefit for people aged 60 or over but for these benefits the £16,000 upper limit will be retained except for those entitled to the guarantee credit.

If you are already getting Income Support in October 2003, you will not need to make a claim for Pension Credit. If you do not receive Income Support, you will need to claim (advance claims can be made from April 2003).

For more information, see Age Concern Factsheet 49 *Pension Credit from October 2003.*

Housing Benefit and Council Tax Benefit

Housing Benefit provides help with rent, and certain service charges, for council, housing association or private tenants. The maximum Housing Benefit you can get is 100 per cent of your rent including service charges. If a heating charge is included in your rent this will not be covered. To qualify for Housing Benefit, you must have savings of £16,000 or less and a low income. If you have a partner, your combined income and savings will be taken into account but the limits will be the same.

Council Tax Benefit provides help with paying the Council Tax. There are two types, known as 'main Council Tax Benefit' and 'second adult rebate'. You may qualify for the former if you have savings of £16,000 or less and a low income. The maximum benefit you can get is 100 per cent of your Council Tax. You may get a second adult rebate of up to 25 per cent if you have one or more adults with a low income living with you, regardless of your income and savings.

To work out whether you qualify for Housing Benefit or Council Tax Benefit, you follow the same steps as with Income Support (see page 19) but this time the savings limit is £16,000.

If your income is the same as or less than your applicable amount, you will normally get all your rent or Council Tax paid (unless there are deductions, for example for ineligible service charges, for other people living in your home or because your rent or Council Tax band is considered too high).

If your income is more than your applicable amount, your benefit will be reduced. Your maximum Housing Benefit is reduced by 65p for every £1 that your income is more than your applicable amount, while your maximum Council Tax Benefit is reduced by 20p for every £1.

If you are claiming Income Support or income-based Jobseeker's Allowance, you can fill in a claim form for Housing Benefit and Council Tax Benefit at the same time. If not, you should get an application form from the Housing and Council Tax Benefit section of your local council.

For more information about Housing Benefit and Council Tax Benefit, see Age Concern Factsheet 17 *Housing Benefit and Council Tax Benefit.*

Other help with Council Tax

In addition to Council Tax Benefit, there are various other ways in which your Council Tax bill may be reduced:

Exemptions Some properties – mainly certain empty ones – are exempt (ie there will be no Council Tax to pay).

Disability reduction scheme Your property may be placed in a lower band if it has certain features which are important for a disabled person. (Properties are all allocated to one of eight bands (A–H) depending on their estimated value.) Properties in the lowest band (A) that have the relevant disability features also qualify for a reduction.

Discounts may be given in some circumstances – for example if you live alone, or if a second person living with you is 'severely mentally impaired' or in some circumstances if they are a carer.

For more information about Council Tax, see Age Concern Factsheet 21 *The Council Tax and older people.*

The Social Fund

The Social Fund provides lump-sum payments to people with low incomes to help with exceptional expenses. These payments are mainly available to people on Income Support, income-based Jobseeker's Allowance and (from October 2003) Pension Credit, but people on Housing Benefit or Council Tax Benefit also qualify for Funeral Payments. Cold Weather Payments and Funeral Payments are mandatory (ie they must be made if you fulfil the qualifying conditions), while Community Care Grants, Budgeting Loans and Crisis Loans are all discretionary. Budgeting Loans and Crisis Loans have to be repaid. For people over 60, the amount of savings over £1,000 will normally be deducted from any grant awarded; for younger people this applies to savings over £500. Budgeting Loans and Crisis Loans must be paid back, but they are interest-free.

 For more information about the Social Fund, see social security guide SB 16.

Other help for people with low incomes

If you receive a benefit such as Income Support, income-based Job-seeker's Allowance or Housing Benefit, you may qualify for certain other benefits, including:

Grants for repairs and improvements In some situations you may be able to receive a grant to help with household repairs or improvements, as described on pages 112–114.

Help with fuel bills There are no regular weekly social security payments towards fuel bills but there are Winter Fuel Payments and Cold Weather Payments.

Winter Fuel Payments provide help with the cost of fuel bills for pensioner households. They are paid to most people aged 60 or over and there are no income or savings limits. If you are aged 60 or over, you will normally receive £100 or £200, depending on your circumstances (you should get £200 if you are the only person in the household entitled to a payment). If you are receiving a State pension, Income Support or certain other benefits, then you should not need to claim as payments will normally be made automatically before Christmas. In other circumstances – for example if you are a man aged 60 not receiving any State benefits – you will need to claim (by 30 March 2003 for the Winter 2002–2003 payment) and should contact your local social security office.

If you receive Income Support or income-based JSA and it includes a pensioner or disability premium, you may be eligible for **Cold Weather Payments**. A payment of £8.50 is made when the average temperature is recorded as, or is forecast to be, 0 degrees Celsius over seven consecutive days.

See page 117 for information on sources of help with heating and insulation.

Grants for insulation and draughtproofing These are explained on page 116.

Help with health costs If you receive Income Support or income-based Jobseeker's Allowance, you will be entitled to help with some health costs, as explained on pages 147–148.

Legal fees If you receive Income Support or income-based Jobseeker's Allowance, or have an income of that level, you may be able to obtain help with legal advice and representation. This may include help with making a will if you are over 70 or you are disabled.

For more information, see Age Concern Factsheet 43 *Obtaining and paying for legal advice.*

Travel concessions These are available to older people on most forms of transport, as described on pages 74–76.

Working Tax Credit This Credit is to be introduced in April 2003. It will be available to employed or self-employed people and there will be no upper age limit for making a claim. There will be a disability element and a 50 plus element.

For more information, contact your local Jobcentre Plus office or Inland Revenue Enquiry Centre or ring the Tax Credits Helpline on 0845 360 3900.

Benefits for people with disabilities and their carers

Incapacity Benefit

Incapacity Benefit (IB) is paid to people who are unable to work because of illness or disability. It depends on NI contributions, but is not usually affected by other income or savings, although for claims since April 2001 a personal or occupational pension of more than £85 a week may reduce benefit. It can normally only be paid to people under pension age when their period of incapacity began.

There are three levels of Incapacity Benefit: **the short-term lower rate** which is paid for up to 28 weeks; **the short-term higher rate** which is paid from 29 to 52 weeks; and **the long-term rate** which is paid after 52 weeks at a weekly rate of £70.95 in 2002–2003.

The short-term lower rate is not taxable; the other rates are. Additional sums are payable if you become disabled before 45. Increases for adult dependants can be paid only for a husband or wife aged 60 or over, depending on their earnings.

To qualify for the short-term lower rate you will normally only need to provide a medical certificate from your doctor stating that you are unable to do your usual job. After 28 weeks you will normally have to undertake a 'personal capability assessment' to decide whether you are capable of doing any work. Since April 2002 you may be required to attend a work-focussed interview as a condition of benefit.

The long-term rate of IB cannot be paid after pension age. So once you reach pension age, you should draw the State Retirement Pension.

If you were receiving Invalidity Benefit on 12 April 1995, you will be covered by transitional rules introduced to provide some protection against reduction in the amount of benefit people received. In this case your benefit will not be taxable.

Disability Living Allowance

Disability Living Allowance (DLA) is for people who become ill or disabled before the age of 65 and make a claim before their 65th birthday. The benefit does not depend on NI contributions, is not affected by income and savings, is paid on top of other benefits or pensions, and is not taxable. It is intended to provide help towards the extra costs arising from illness or disability, but you don't have to use it to buy care: it is up to you how you spend it.

DLA has two parts, a care component and a mobility component:

The care component is for people who need help with personal care, supervision, or to have someone watching over them. It is paid at three levels (£56.25, £37.65 and £14.90 in 2002–2003; £57.20, £38.30 and £15.15 in 2003–2004). People who need help with 'bodily functions' (for example eating, moving around or going to the toilet), or who require continual supervision during the day and the night, receive the higher level; those who need such help during either the day or the night receive the middle level; those who need help for a significant portion of the day get the lower level.

The mobility component is paid at two different levels (£39.30 and £14.90 in 2002–2003; £39.95 and £15.15 in 2003–2004). People who cannot walk or have great difficulty walking receive the higher level, while people who need someone with them when walking outside receive the lower level.

For information about the Motability scheme and other concessions for people who receive the mobility component of DLA, see pages 79–80.

Attendance Allowance

Attendance Allowance is for disabled people aged 65 or over. It is paid at two levels: both the rates and the criteria are the same as for the higher and middle levels on the care component of DLA. There are day and/or night conditions but there is no mobility component.

For more information, see Age Concern Factsheet 34 *Attendance Allowance and Disability Living Allowance.*

Invalid Care Allowance

This benefit, which is being renamed Carer's Allowance from April 2003, is for people who care for a severely disabled person for at least 35 hours a week. The weekly rate is £42.45 in 2002–2003, plus £25.35 for an adult dependant (depending on their income). In 2003–2004 the figures will be £43.15 and £25.80. There is no upper age limit for claiming the allowance. It is taxable.

Invalid Care Allowance (ICA) does not depend on NI contributions, but you cannot receive it if your earnings are over a certain limit or if you receive certain other benefits. The person you look after must receive Attendance Allowance, the higher or middle level of the care component of DLA, or Constant Attendance Allowance.

If you are receiving ICA when you reach pension age, it will be adjusted to take account of any Retirement Pension you draw. If your pension is less than £42.45, then the allowance will be reduced by the amount of pension received. If your pension is more than £42.45 you may still qualify for ICA because of the 'underlying entitlement' rules – you won't actually get the benefit called ICA but you may get help from other means-tested benefits like Housing or Council Tax Benefit.

You can get a factsheet and further advice about ICA from Carers UK at the address on page 195. For more details about benefits for people with disabilities, see *The Disability Rights Handbook*, which is published by the Disability Alliance (address on page 177).

Your tax position

Under the UK tax system people are assessed annually to determine whether they are liable to pay any tax for that tax year (the tax year runs from 6 April one year to 5 April the following year). There are three main taxes payable by individuals: Income Tax, Capital Gains Tax and Inheritance Tax. While evading tax is against the law, avoiding tax – ie, arranging your affairs so that you pay as little tax as possible – is both legal and sensible. This section gives a brief outline of how the tax system works.

> The Inland Revenue is the government department responsible for these three taxes. Inland Revenue leaflet IR 121 is called *Income Tax and pensioners*. Details of how to obtain Inland Revenue leaflets are given on page 178.

Income Tax

Factfile

■ People aged over 65 pay Income Tax if their income is more than £117 a week.

■ Only around half of people aged over 60 pay Income Tax.

■ Nearly one and a half million pensioners pay their tax through the self-assessment system.

You are allowed a certain amount of income each year without paying tax on it at all. The rest of your income is taxed, and the bigger your income the higher the rate of tax you pay on it.

In 2002–2003 there are four rates of tax:

■ Up to £1,920 – 10 per cent (starting rate)
■ £1,921 to £29,900 – 22 per cent (basic rate) or 20 per cent on interest
■ Over £29,900 – 40 per cent (higher rate)

Income Tax is paid on what you earn and on what you receive as a pension or from investments. Some income is not taxable (ie, is ignored completely), including many social security benefits, gifts and the first £30,000 of any redundancy payment.

Your liability for Income Tax (and Capital Gains Tax) is assessed annually by your tax office: your employer's tax office, if you are still in paid work; your last employer's tax office, if you are unemployed or retired; or the tax office covering your business, if you are self-employed. If you are self-employed, you are responsible for declaring your earnings to the Inland Revenue. Tax is calculated on the income you receive in the current tax year.

If you are self-employed or a higher-rate taxpayer or have received some untaxed income, you will normally be sent a tax return each year. Under the system of self-assessment introduced in April 1997, you can choose whether to calculate the amount of tax yourself or let the Inland Revenue do it. If you want the Inland Revenue to do it, you must send the completed tax return by 30 September; if you calculate tax yourself, you have until 31 January to do it and to pay the amount outstanding. If you are late, you may incur penalties.

All taxpayers are obliged by law to keep records of their income and capital gains. If you are not usually sent a tax return but have a new source of income or capital gain on which you need to pay tax, you must tell the Inland Revenue.

For further information, see Inland Revenue leaflet SA/BK8 *Self-assessment: your guide* or contact the Revenue's Self-Assessment Helpline on 0845 9000 444.

How income is taxed

Most income is taxed before you receive it.

Earnings and occupational and personal pensions Tax is generally collected through the Pay As You Earn (PAYE) system. The tax is deducted by your employer or the pension scheme or annuity provider. They work out the tax due using a tax code provided by the Inland Revenue. It is important to check that your tax code, and the amount of tax you have paid, are right.

For more information, see Inland Revenue leaflets *Pay As You Earn (PAYE)* and P3 *Understanding your tax code.*

State Pensions The State Pension is taxable but it is paid without tax being deducted. The tax on it is collected from your earnings or your pension by changing your tax code. If the State Pension is your only source of income, it is unlikely that you will have to pay any tax.

Savings income Interest on savings or investment is mostly paid with 20 per cent tax already deducted. If you are a non-taxpayer, or liable for tax only on some of the income, you should be able to reclaim the tax. However, you should note that non-taxpayers cannot reclaim the 10 per cent tax deducted from dividends on shares and some unit trusts. If you are a higher-rate taxpayer, you will have more tax to pay. Where income is paid gross (ie, before tax is deducted), as with most National Savings accounts, you will be sent a self-assessment tax form to account for the tax due.

Calculating your Income Tax

To work out whether you will have to pay Income Tax, or to check that you are paying the correct amount, you need to do the following:

1 **Add together all your income for the year** You need not include income that is tax-free (see above). To add up your total gross income, you will need to 'gross up' any income received with tax already deducted. For example, if you received £800 building society interest after tax at 20 per cent has been deducted, this is equivalent to £1,000 gross income (ie, you divide by 4 and multiply by 5).

All investment income is taxed at 20 per cent for basic-rate taxpayers (except dividends from shares, and some unit trusts or Open-ended Investment Companies (OEICs), that are taxed at 10 per cent). Higher-rate taxpayers will have to pay more. Income from investments always 'sits on the top' of your income – so the allowance or the tax always applies first to your other income and then to income from investments.

2 Find out what tax allowances you are entitled to Everyone has a Personal Allowance; ie, they are allowed to have a certain amount of income before they have to pay tax on it.

The Personal Allowance is set at different levels depending on your age (and, if you are 65 or over, on your income). In 2002–2003 they are:

- £4,615 for people aged under 65;
- £6,100 for people aged between 65 and 74; or
- £6,370 for people aged 75 or more.

A Married Couple's Allowance is also available for couples where the older partner was born before 6 April 1935. It is simply a 10 per cent reduction in the tax that is due. The allowances in 2002–2003 are £5,465 (deduction of £546.50) if the older partner is aged 67 to 74 or £5,535 (deduction of £553.50) if aged 75 or more.

You may get other allowances too that allow you to receive a certain amount of income without paying Income Tax. If your income is less than your allowance(s), you do not pay any tax. You cannot, however, be paid any 'unused' allowance.

If your income is over a certain limit (£17,900 in 2002–2003), the higher Personal Allowances for older people are gradually reduced (by £1 for each £2 over the limit) to the level of the basic allowance. The Married Couple's Allowance is similarly reduced if your income is over a certain level.

Other tax allowances include the Blind Person's Allowance and the Children's Tax Credit. Tax allowances and rates for the following tax year are normally announced each year in the Budget.

3 Deduct your Personal Allowance from your total income This gives you the amount of your income on which tax must be paid, known as your 'taxable income'.

4 Work out the tax you should pay Using the 2002–2003 tax rates, take 10 per cent of your taxable income up to £1,920, 22 per cent of your income from £1,921 to £29,900, and 40 per cent of any income over that amount, and add the three figures together. (Note the paragraph on page 30 about income from investments.) If you receive a Married Couple's Allowance or other allowance that provides 10 per cent tax relief, calculate 10 per cent of this allowance. Deduct this amount from the tax you are due to pay to give your total tax bill.

For more information, see the Age Concern annual publication *Your Taxes and Savings* (details on page 198) or Factsheet 15 *Income Tax and older people.*

Cutting down Income Tax

Transferring savings or investments between husband and wife A couple may be able to save tax by transferring savings to the partner who pays no tax or tax at a lower rate.

Married Couple's Allowance This allowance is normally taken off the husband's tax bill. However, he can transfer the allowance if his income is too low to make use of it, or a couple can choose to transfer some of it. Inland Revenue form 18 explains about transferring the allowance.

Personal pensions You get full tax relief on contributions, so taking out a personal pension is a good way to lower your tax bill if you are still earning.

Bank and building society accounts Non-taxpayers can apply to have interest paid gross (ie, before tax is deducted), rather than having to reclaim tax at the end of the financial year.

 For information on tax-free investments, see pages 38–39 and 43–44.

Capital Gains Tax

You may have to pay some Capital Gains Tax (CGT) if you sell or give away an asset which has increased in value since you bought it. An 'asset' is something you own, such as shares, antiques or property. However, not all profits are taxed. A certain amount of profit (£7,700 in 2002–2003) is exempt each year (spouses are taxed independently on any gains, so husbands and wives have an exempt amount of £7,700 each).

Any gift between husband and wife is entirely free of CGT (provided that they do not then dispose of the asset). In addition, some items are free of CGT, including:

- your home (provided it has been your 'main' private residence throughout your ownership);
- private cars, and personal possessions worth up to £6,000 each;
- National Savings certificates and most British Government stocks;
- gifts to registered charities; and
- proceeds from most life insurance policies.

Any 'chargeable gain' above the £7,700 limit is added to your income and taxed as though it was sitting on top of your income.

For more information about CGT, see Inland Revenue leaflet CGT1 *Capital Gains Tax: an introduction* or contact your tax office.

Inheritance Tax

Inheritance Tax (IHT) may have to be paid on what you leave to your heirs or give away in the seven years before your death. However, IHT is not payable on any assets left to a husband or wife, or if your estate (plus gifts made over the past seven years, excluding those that are tax-free) is worth less than £250,000 (2002–2003 limit) after debts and reasonable funeral expenses have been paid. IHT is payable at 40 per cent on any amount over the limit.

Certain gifts are exempt from IHT, whether or not you survive seven years after making them.

Reducing IHT

For people who can afford to, the easiest way to avoid your heirs having to pay IHT is to make lifetime gifts early or to keep them within the exemption limits. However, don't try to give away something but continue to benefit from it – for example if you give your house to your children but continue to live in it, the value will still count as part of your estate.

Trusts can be a way to avoid IHT but they are expensive to set up and run and trust law is extremely complicated, so seek professional advice first. Some insurance companies and financial consultants market plans to reduce or avoid IHT; they too are complicated and are generally best avoided.

For more information about IHT, see Inland Revenue leaflet IHT3 *Inheritance Tax: an introduction.*

Your savings and investments

Deciding what to do with your savings is never a straightforward matter. The safest investments may not be the most profitable. You will often get better returns by agreeing to tie your money up for a period of years, but you may need access to at least some of your savings for possible emergencies. In addition to whatever you may have saved over the years, when you retire you may receive part of your pension as a lump sum, and you may decide to invest at least part of this. This section looks at some of the savings and investment options, with the aim of helping you choose those best suited to your particular needs.

Try to have a 'portfolio' of different savings and investments as it is safer not to have all your eggs in one basket, and one product is unlikely to meet all your needs anyway. Before investing, think about your circumstances, the amount you have to invest, your attitude to risk, your tax position and how long you can afford to have your money tied up. Always keep part of your savings available for emergencies. Check interest rates before you invest and read all the conditions attached to the financial product you are interested in.

Advice and protection for investors

The Financial Services Authority (FSA) now regulates almost all investment and savings products as well as the people who sell them and the banks and financial companies that back them.

The products that are *outside* the scope of the FSA include National Savings products as well as current and savings accounts with banks and building societies. If you buy shares directly yourself, this is not covered by the FSA but the adviser or broker you buy them through will be. Also excluded are investments in physical things like property, antiques and cars. Mortgage advice and general insurance will be regulated by the FSA in 2004.

Getting financial advice

Many different experts give advice on money matters, including actuaries, accountants, bank managers, insurance salespeople, solicitors and stockbrokers. The way that financial advisers work is changing. Under the plans there will be three sorts of financial adviser:

■ **Independent financial advisers (IFAs)** who have to offer the most suitable product from the whole marketplace. They will not earn commission but will have to charge fees.

■ **Distributors** (although they may not be called this) who will sell a range of products and who will still make their money through commission.

■ **Tied representatives** who will sell their own company's products and those of a few competitor companies.

It is illegal for anyone to offer most financial advice – or to provide access to investment products – without being registered. You can check if a person is registered with the FSA at the address on page 177. The FSA publishes a free booklet called *Guide to financial advice*, which gives tips on avoiding bad investments.

You can get a list of IFAs in your area from the Internet on www.ifap.org.uk or www.sofa.org or www.searchifa.co.uk or you can ring IFA Promotions Ltd at the number on page 177. However, personal recommendation is usually the best way to find a financial adviser.

Regulations affecting financial advisers

Advisers selling regulated financial products have to follow certain procedures.

Disclosure of commission They have to tell you exactly how much commission they are getting. Companies that do not pay commission to staff must give a comparable figure, taking account of factors such as a proportion of the salesperson's basic salary.

Key features of the product The adviser must tell you about the aims, risks and benefits and about charges and expenses.

A personal illustration The adviser must show the product's projected costs and its likely growth based on your personal circumstances.

Reason why the product is appropriate The adviser must write a letter explaining why the product is right for you.

Cooling off You normally have a period in which you can cancel without penalty. The adviser must tell you clearly what this cooling off period is.

Making a complaint

If you want to make a complaint, you should first write to the Chief Executive of the company. If your complaint is not then dealt with to your satisfaction within eight weeks, you can go to the Financial Ombudsman Service (FOS). You can complain to FOS about any financial firm – such as a bank or investment company – that is registered with the FSA, even if the product (such as a current account) is not itself regulated by the FSA. The service is free.

For more information, contact FOS at the address on page 177.

Banks and building societies

Putting money into a bank or building society account is a very 'safe' form of saving. The capital remains intact and can easily be withdrawn, and you receive interest. The disadvantage is that if you take out the interest as it is paid, you will have left only the money you started with – the value of your savings will not keep up with inflation.

The distinction between banks and building societies has now almost disappeared. The only difference is that with a building society all the profits go back into the society; with a bank, some of the profits are distributed to shareholders. However, it doesn't always work out that building societies offer a better deal.

Banks and building societies usually offer a variety of accounts, including:

Current accounts, which now offer interest on your balance. If your bank or building society doesn't pay interest on your current account, you could move it to one that does. It is now much easier to change your current account as your old bank has to co-operate fully with your new one to facilitate the move. The best rates are paid on accounts which are run over the Internet or using the phone. Even if you prefer to use a bank where you can visit a branch, rates do vary greatly. Overdraft interest rates also vary – they are very high and higher still for unauthorised overdrafts.

Savings accounts are becoming increasingly similar to current accounts (Internet current accounts often offer better rates of interest than most savings accounts). To choose the best for you, look at the rate of interest and think whether you need the interest paid monthly or annually and how long you want the money tied up for.

Fixed rate accounts guarantee you that your money will pay a fixed return for a fixed period of, for example, 5.5 per cent over two years. You have to agree to leave your money in for that length of time. If interest rates fall, you will do well, but if they rise, you may end up with a poor return.

Cash ISAs (Individual Savings Accounts) replaced TESSAs (Tax Exempt Special Savings Accounts) and PEPs (Personal Equity Plans) in 1999. You can put £3,000 each tax year into a cash ISA (Individual Savings Account), which is sometimes called a mini-cash ISA. It is a savings account on which interest is paid, but the interest is tax-free and the interest rates tend to be higher than for other accounts. (For information on shares ISAs, see page 43.)

MoneyFacts is a monthly publication giving interest rates for all financial institutions. It also gives details of overdraft terms. For more information, see the address on page 178 or ask at your local library.

National Savings

The Government backs National Savings and so its savings and investment products are as 'safe' as you can get. Some products are tax-free and so are good for taxpayers. Others pay the interest gross and so non-taxpayers don't have to worry about reclaiming deducted tax, and taxpayers keep their money until they sort out their tax at the end of the year.

Certificates offer tax-free capital growth over a fixed period of two or five years. If you cash them in early, you will be charged a stiff penalty. At the end of the period you should reinvest the money or take it out; if you do not, you will only earn a special rate of interest called the General Extension Rate, which is very low. Some certificates are 'index-linked', which means that they pay an interest rate which is a fixed amount above the rate of inflation (they are thus attractive if you think that inflation is going to rise).

Bonds If you are over 60, you can get a regular monthly income and a reasonable rate of interest from pensioner bonds. Income bonds are similar for younger people. The rate of interest is guaranteed for one, two or five years. Capital bonds offer guaranteed growth over one, three or five years. In all cases there are penalties for early withdrawal.

Premium bonds don't have a good rate of return but the prizes are tax-free, so higher-rate taxpayers may find them attractive.

You can get the *Investor's guide* and other free leaflets about National Savings from some post offices or by phoning 0645 645 000 or looking at the website at www.nationalsavings.co.uk

Government stock

If you buy government stock (generally known as 'gilt-edged securities' or 'gilts'), you lend your money to the Government and it guarantees to give you it all back at a certain time and meanwhile pays you interest at a fixed rate. The interest is normally paid in two instalments each year. It is taxable but is normally paid gross and you will have to account for the tax and pay it through self-assessment.

Initially, the Government sells gilts in certificates with what is called a 'nominal' value of £100. The certificate has a 'redemption date', which is the date on which the holder will be repaid £100 for it, and a 'coupon', which is the name for the rate of interest paid on that £100 each year.

For example, 7¾ per cent Treasury stock 2006 promises to pay the holder of a £100 certificate £7.75 a year in two instalments on 8 March and 8 September and redeem the certificates by repaying the £100 on 8 September 2006.

To get a £100 certificate you may have to pay more than £100. If you bought for £112, for example, you would still get £7.75 a year which would work out at a return on your £112 of 6.45 per cent. That figure is known as its 'running yield' and roughly equates to the annual return on your money.

When the stock reaches its redemption date, you will only get £100 back for your £112, however. So to work out your 'redemption yield' (ie, a measure of the real overall return on your money) the £12 must be taken off your interest payments. You also need to take account of the fact that money now is worth more than money tomorrow. This is complex but the price of gilts generally reflects their value in the light of expectations about interest rates. The *Financial Times* and some other broadsheet papers publish lists of all government stock each day, together with their running and redemption yields.

What stocks you buy will depend on whether you are more interested in income or in capital gain. You could, for example, buy a high-coupon stock and accept a small capital loss at redemption. If you are a higher-rate taxpayer, you may be better off with a low-coupon stock and make a capital gain which is tax-free at redemption.

Gilts can be bought and sold through banks, some building societies, stockbrokers and also by post on a form available at post offices. The commission has to be taken into account when working out the yield on your money.

 You can find out more about gilts from the Debt Management Office (DMO) at the address on page 176. The DMO administers gilts for the Government and produces a free guide for private investors.

Investing in companies

Shares

For most people, investment implies buying shares in companies – ie, investing in the stock market. A 'share' is a share in the ownership of the company. Shareholders get part of the company's profits as a 'dividend', as well as any gain made when they sell their shares. However, the value of shares can go down as well as up.

Stocks and shares are bought and sold on the Stock Exchange and their prices vary from day to day. There is always a risk involved when putting money in the stock market, so it is usually best to get professional advice. If you want to pick your shares yourself, you need to keep an eye on your investment all the time. Read the financial press and remember to diversify to reduce risk.

You cannot buy shares directly – you have to go through a broker. The cost of buying and selling has fallen recently, particularly for smaller telephone, internet or postal deals. Many banks or building societies offer a cheap dealing service. In addition to the broker's fee, you pay stamp duty of 0.5 per cent on all share purchases.

If you do invest money in the stock market, make sure that it is money that you can do without for a number of years (five at least and preferably ten or more) – it is a long-term investment.

Corporate bonds

These are loans to a company in exchange for a fixed and guaranteed rate of interest and your capital back at the end of a fixed period. There is less risk than with shares, as the value of the investment remains the same and interest is guaranteed. But there is still a risk – the company may go bust and default on its payments. You can minimise this risk by investing in a fund which holds corporate bonds in a range of companies. These are done through a unit trust (see below).

Indirect investments

Unit trusts

Because the value of shares in individual companies is so unpredictable, most people put their money into a fund which has shares in a wide range of companies. These funds are usually sold through 'unit trusts'. You normally buy a number of 'units' in this fund and get a return depending on the overall growth of the money in the fund. Some funds pay out these gains as income, while others just let it accumulate and you have to sell units to realise money from your investment.

Most funds are 'actively managed' by a team who move the money around to try to get the best returns. 'Passive' funds, on the other hand, simply buy shares in all the companies in a particular stock market index (such as the FTSE 100 for example). They are sometimes called 'tracker' funds and their costs are much lower than for active funds. They will probably do just as well as managed funds in the long term and the charges are a major consideration in choosing a fund. Picking one that will perform well in the future is largely a matter of luck.

You can buy unit trusts either with a lump sum (usually of £500 or more) or with regular savings starting at around £25 a month. You can buy unit trusts through an ISA for a tax-free return. Prices are published in the papers and financial magazines – the lower or 'bid' price is the one at which you sell back the units to the company; the higher or 'offer' price is the one at which you buy them. Only buy unit trusts from a firm that is regulated by the Financial Services Authority.

For more information, see the factsheet on unit trusts, which is available from the Investment Management Association at the address on page 178.

Investment trusts

An alternative to a unit trust is to buy a share in an investment trust. These are companies which invest in the shares of other companies.

Investment trusts are freer to take risks than unit trusts and so the value of the shares is more likely to go up and down. They are not regulated by the FSA. There are more than 300 investment trust companies to choose from and you can invest from £25 a month.

 For more information about investment trusts, contact the Association of Investment Trust Companies at the address on page 176.

Open-ended Investment Companies (OEICs)

OEICs may eventually replace unit trusts and investment trusts. An OEIC is a company which invests in shares, and investors in the OEIC buy a share in the company. They are simpler and cheaper, and, like unit trusts, they are 'open ended'; ie, there is no limit to the total amount you can invest. Unlike investment trusts, they are regulated by the FSA.

Shares in an OEIC carry a single price at which they are bought and sold, so there is no expensive spread. The share price moves up and down in line with the stock market, so an OEIC, like any other share investment, is for the long term.

 For more information about OEICs, contact the Investment Management Association at the address on page 178.

Tax-free investments

Individual Savings Accounts (ISAs) are the one way to invest tax-free since April 1999 when they replaced PEPs (Personal Equity Plans). An ISA is not an investment in itself but simply a way of holding an investment so that it is free of all tax. The maximum amount you can invest through an ISA is £7,000 a year. All of that can go into a shares ISA, unless you have already put money into a cash ISA (see page 38), in which case you are limited to £3,000 in shares.

Purchased life annuities are not the same as the annuity you have to buy with your pension fund (see page 15) as they are treated differently for tax purposes. With a pension fund annuity, the whole of the income is treated as taxable income. With a purchased life annuity, part of the money you get each month is treated simply as a return of your capital and not taxed (only the interest you are earning is taxed). The Inland Revenue decides how much is taxed depending on your age and sex; the older you are, the more of your money is tax-free. The minimum sum required is around £5,000 and the difference between annuities is considerable, so shop around carefully.

Other indirect investments

Investment bonds are single-premium life assurance policies. Your money is invested in a separate fund of pooled investments, rather like a unit trust. The attraction of these bonds is the tax-deferred income they provide, which can be particularly useful if you need to keep your tax bill down to qualify for the higher age-related Personal Allowances (see page 31).

Guaranteed income and growth bonds are run by insurance companies for a fixed term and at a fixed rate. With an income bond, you invest a lump sum for one to five years and get a fixed income, usually paid yearly, and return of your capital after an agreed period. Where the income from the bond is compounded and paid at the end of the agreed time, it is known as a guaranteed growth bond. These give a return only when they are cashed in. Interest on both types of bond is paid net of tax; the tax is not reclaimable even by non-taxpayers.

 For more information about investments, see Age Concern Books' annual publication *Your Taxes and Savings* (details on page 198).

Making a will

Many people never make a will, yet it is the only way to ensure that your assets are disposed of as you wish after your death. It also makes things much easier for whoever has to sort out your affairs. Anyone over the age of 18 can make a will, provided they have 'testamentary capacity' – ie, that they fully understand what they are doing.

Factfile

- It is estimated that about 70 per cent of adults in England have not made a will.

How to make a will

Most agencies advise going to a solicitor even for a simple will as problems can arise after your death if a bequest is not entirely clear. However, you can make your will yourself and pre-printed will forms can be bought from stationers very cheaply. If you do make your own will, make sure that you:

- say that this will revokes all others (even if you have never made a will before);
- decide who will be your executor(s) – ie, the person(s) named in the will to administer your affairs after your death;
- choose who will be the main beneficiary of your estate – ie, the person (or people) who will receive the remainder ('residue') of your estate after any specific bequests have been made; and
- make provision in case any beneficiary dies before you do.

It is good idea to choose two executors in case one dies before you. Executors can be beneficiaries of the estate. People normally choose their spouse or children, but you can choose a professional such as a solicitor or bank manager (ask about their charges before appointing a professional).

Your signature to the will must be witnessed by two independent people (not your spouse or anyone who stands to inherit or their spouse).

You can keep your will at home or it can be lodged with a solicitor or bank (banks may charge for this service). A will can also be lodged with the Probate Department at the Principal Registry of the Family Division (address on page 179). A fee of £15 is charged when a will is deposited. The main thing is to make sure that all concerned know where to find it.

Going to a solicitor

It is advisable to go to a solicitor unless your will is very simple, especially if you intend to leave significant sums to people other then those who might expect to inherit, such as your spouse and children. If you do not already have a solicitor, the Citizen Advice Bureau (CAB) may be able to help you find one. The public library may have a directory listing solicitors by area. It is a good idea to ask at the outset what the cost will be as it varies according to the complexity of the will.

If you are over 70, or disabled, and have a low income and little savings, you may qualify for help with making your will – ask your CAB for further details.

In addition to solicitors, financial institutions such as banks, building societies and insurance companies can now prepare wills. There are also will-writing services available, such as that offered by Age Concern England.

Dying intestate

If you die without making a will – known as dying intestate – your estate will be distributed to members of your family according to certain rules: a husband or wife will receive at least the first £125,000, but surviving children or grandchildren will receive some of the estate if it exceeds £125,000. If you are not married, your parents or nearest relatives will inherit. Dying intestate could, in certain circumstances, mean your spouse having to sell the home you share.

Revising your will

If you marry or remarry, your will automatically becomes invalid and should be revised (unless you were intending to marry when the will was made and it refers to your proposed marriage). Divorce does not automatically make a will invalid. Codicils (supplements to a will) can be added to an existing will for minor changes. For major changes you should make a new will revoking the former one. Alterations should never be made on the original document.

For more information, see Age Concern Factsheet 7 *Making your will.*

Other arrangements to be made in the event of death

If you have strong feelings about the arrangements for your funeral – burial or cremation, type of ceremony, etc – you can leave written instructions with your will.

Funerals are expensive. If you want to ensure that enough money is readily available to cover the cost, this can be done by means of a special bank or building society account, a life assurance policy or a prepayment plan. The National Association of Funeral Directors (address on page 196) and Age Concern England offer prepayment plans, as do some friendly societies and a few insurance companies.

See Age Concern Factsheet 27 *Arranging a funeral* for further information, details about the Social Fund Funeral Payments for people who receive certain means-tested benefits and a list of organisations that offer pre-payment plans.

There are certain personal papers that whoever sorts out another person's affairs after their death will need to find. It is a good idea, therefore, if such papers are kept together. Apart from the will, these include:

■ details of pensions, insurance policies, investments, bank and building society accounts, credit arrangements, credit cards;
■ property deeds, lease, mortgage details, rent book; and
■ addresses of tax office and professional advisers.

Age Concern publishes a leaflet called *Instructions for My Next of Kin and Executors upon My Death*. It can be left in a convenient place to tell your family where all your important documents are, including your will. The leaflet is available from the address on page 204.

Managing another person's money

You may at some point find that you have to take over the management of someone else's money – perhaps that of a parent or other older relative – either permanently or temporarily. In some circumstances you may be asked for help; if the other person goes into hospital, for example, or needs help with a specific legal transaction such as buying or selling a house. But you might sometimes have to take over without consent; for example, if the other person suffers from dementia or a severe form of mental illness.

If the person is mentally competent

Informal arrangements

There are several informal arrangements that can be made by people who are still mentally competent and would like someone else to act on their behalf. Any such arrangement automatically becomes invalid if the person whose affairs you are handling becomes mentally incapable of understanding the arrangement.

Third party mandate Someone who is physically unable to get to the bank or building society may authorise you to use their account. This is known as a 'third party mandate'.

Opening a joint account This gives you easy access to the funds held in the account. For anyone who opens a joint account with someone other than their spouse, it is advisable to have a written agreement signed by all the account holders confirming their intentions.

Acting as an agent If you collect a social security benefit or pension from the post office on behalf of another person (the 'claimant'), you are acting as their 'agent'. If the arrangement is a temporary one, claimant and agent simply complete the form on the back of the order. If you are likely to be acting as agent for a long time, you can get an agency card from the local social security office.

Appointing an attorney

If someone (the 'donor') wishes to make more formal arrangements for another person (the 'attorney') to act on their behalf, he or she can make a power of attorney. A power of attorney is a legal document that authorises you to act on the donor's behalf and shows the extent of your powers.

A power of attorney can be made by anyone who is mentally capable of understanding what they are doing. Donors can appoint anyone they choose to be their attorney. This does not affect their right to act for themselves as long as they remain mentally capable.

There are two main types of power of attorney:

■ an Ordinary Power of Attorney (used while the donor is physically incapable of managing their affairs, for example because of illness or because they are going abroad for a long time); and

■ an Enduring Power of Attorney (see below).

Both of these can be either general (giving the attorney 'blank' powers to act on the donor's behalf) or limited to specific powers (for example to buy or sell a house). If the power is to be limited rather than general, it needs to be carefully worded, preferably in consultation with a solicitor.

If someone is looking forward to future events, then they should consider an Enduring Power of Attorney.

An Enduring Power of Attorney (EPA)

An EPA is a legal document by which someone appoints one or more persons to act for them, should they in the future become incapable of managing for themselves. As with the Ordinary Power of Attorney, it must be executed (ie, signed) while the donor is capable of understanding the nature and effect of creating an EPA. An EPA must be in a form prescribed by law. The form may be purchased from a law stationer or drawn up by a solicitor.

It is advisable to appoint more than one attorney to act jointly and severally (which means that they may act together or separately, as they choose). If the attorneys can only act jointly, it will mean that on the death or incapacity of one of the two, the EPA will expire. If only one attorney is appointed and something happens to that person, the donor may not be able to create a fresh EPA.

If you are acting as an attorney under an enduring power, you have a duty to register the power with the Public Guardianship Office once you consider that the donor is, or is becoming, mentally disordered.

When trying to decide when someone is 'mentally incapable', you should always assume they are capable until they demonstrate otherwise, for example by consistently losing money and failing to pay bills. People with diagnosed mental health problems such as schizophrenia may be temporarily incapable of managing their affairs. If in doubt, always ask for an opinion from the family doctor.

For further information and advice about Enduring Powers of Attorney and how to register them, contact the Public Guardianship Office at the address on page 179.

If the person is mentally incapable

Unless an Enduring Power of Attorney has been made, none of the arrangements described so far will remain legally valid if the person you are acting for becomes mentally incapable of understanding what is going on. There are various formal arrangements that can be made in these circumstances. Often this will involve applying to the Court of Protection to take over the person's financial affairs; but if the person you want to act for has limited income and savings, this may not be necessary.

Claiming benefits and pensions as appointee A representative of the Department for Work and Pensions (usually the decision-maker in the local social security office) can appoint another person (the 'appointee') to collect a social security benefit or pension on someone else's (the claimant's) behalf and to spend it on their needs. A close relative who lives with or visits the claimant frequently will usually be preferred. If the claimant has made a power of attorney or an Enduring Power of Attorney, the attorney should be appointed.

Further information for appointees (or agents) is provided in social security leaflet GL 21.

Collecting other pensions or payments Similar arrangements can sometimes be made for the appointee to collect and spend a pension or other work-related payment (for example from a government department or the armed forces).

Collecting tax refunds Tax refunds below a certain amount may sometimes be paid to the next of kin of people who are mentally incapable of managing their own affairs.

Using someone else's bank or building society account This may be possible – for example to make withdrawals to provide for their immediate needs – if they have only a small amount of savings. If the bank or building society refuses, you can apply to the Court of Protection to use the account.

The Court of Protection and the Public Guardianship Office

The Court of Protection looks after the financial affairs of people who are unable to manage for themselves because of 'mental disorder'. The Protection Division of the Public Guardianship Office (formerly the Public Trust Office) is responsible for the day-to-day administration of cases under the jurisdiction of the Court of Protection and for registering EPAs.

The Court of Protection can appoint a 'Receiver' (usually a close friend or relative) to deal with the day-to-day management of the patient's financial affairs. A professional adviser such as a solicitor or accountant can be appointed, but they will usually charge a fee. The Public Guardianship Office (PGO) will first assess the client's ('patient's') needs. In most cases the Court of Protection is only involved on the appointment of the Receiver and overseeing the administration of the receivership is the responsibility of the PGO, which has to approve transactions in advance.

 For more information, see Age Concern Factsheet 22 *Legal arrangements for managing financial affairs*. As Scottish law is different from English law, a Scottish version of the factsheet is also available from Freephone 0800 00 99 66.

Making the most of your time

When you retire, all the time previously occupied by work – including travelling, and perhaps doing extra work in the evening – is yours to spend as you choose.

People retiring today can expect to spend nearly as long in retirement as they did at work. Retirement can amount to one third of your life or more. The very word 'retirement' is becoming an anachronism: nowadays the term 'third age' is increasingly used.

The fact that you have so much time at your disposal over so long a period makes it all the more crucial to make good use of it. In this period of life many people discover talents and skills they never knew they had.

- Learning opportunities
- Community involvement
- Earning money in retirement
- Travel
- Going on holiday

Learning opportunities

> **Factfile**
>
> ■ In 2001, 22 per cent of people aged 65–74, and 12 per cent of people aged over 75, took part in some sort of adult learning.

In retirement you can set your own goals. You can study or pursue an interest simply because you want to. You may choose to study for your own personal satisfaction, or indeed in order to learn a specific skill that will increase your earning potential. You may want to study informally or you may hope to take examinations and gain qualifications. You may see going to a class largely as a way of meeting congenial people. Whatever you are hoping to get out of further study or a new pastime, there are a great many opportunities open to people in retirement.

Informal ways of learning

Local libraries are a good place to start to find out what is going on in your area. They may also run their own activities and be able to help with research into local history for example. They are increasingly setting up 'open learning' centres where you can learn to use computers for example and have access to the Internet.

Museums and galleries In addition to visiting a museum or gallery, you may find that the education department provides a programme of courses, lectures and events for interested adults.

Radio and television Many radio and television programmes are, in the widest sense, educational. In addition, many specifically educational programmes are broadcast, sometimes at night, and are often accompanied by cassettes, videos and books. This is a particularly good way of learning a language, for example. For those with cable and satellite TV, there is a wide range of informative programmes – the Discovery Channel, for example, focuses largely on different parts of the world and on nature programmes.

Computers and the Internet

You may be very experienced with information technology already. If you have access to the Internet at home or at your local library or cyber café, there is no limit to the subjects you can learn about. If you always include words such as *tutorial, guides, master class* or *tips* in the query box when you carry out a search, you should find useful sites.

If you are new to computers and would like to find a course to learn how to use them, whether for research or because you want to keep in touch through email, help to run a club or write your life story for example, try to find one that suits your needs.

Hairnet is an organisation which offers computer and Internet training to the over-50s. It has a UK-wide network of older trainers. For more information, contact Hairnet at the address on page 182.

Age Resource has a network of 'desks', based within Age Concern offices or shops, which provide a venue for computer taster sessions. You can contact Age Resource at the address on page 179.

For more information about computers, see the Age Concern Books publications, *Getting the Most from your Computer* and *How to be a Silver Surfer* (details on pages 199 and 200).

Attending classes locally

One of the easiest ways of extending your education in retirement is to go to a class near your home. Almost all learning activities are provided locally, either by statutory, voluntary or commercial bodies. What is available therefore varies from area to area and you will probably need to contact local agencies to find your nearest activities.

Local authority adult education services usually offer a wide variety of classes (academic, vocational, physical and practical – on subjects as diverse as English literature, computer studies, keep fit and cake decorating for example). Some classes lead to recognised qualifications. Prospectuses are usually available in August each year. Fees vary, but there are generally concessionary rates for pensioners, although you may have to ask for them. Many local authorities offer educational guidance services for adults where you can discuss your particular needs.

Workers' Educational Association (WEA) classes tend to be more academic than those run by local authorities. There are more than 1,000 branches in Britain. You can obtain the address of your local branch from the library or local authority education office or from the national office (address on page 188).

University of the Third Age (U3A) (national office address on page 187). The term 'university' is misleading: no qualifications or exams are involved. People join U3A groups to study a wide range of topics, not all of them academic. All activities are arranged by the members themselves.

The National Adult School Organisation (address on page 183) organises local study groups which meet, often in members' homes, weekly or fortnightly, as well as one-day and residential schools locally and nationally.

The Pre-Retirement Association (PRA) (address on page 185) promotes the development of courses and materials for pre-retirement education. The national office is the centre of a network for local PRA groups.

Learndirect is a national adult learning helpline which gives information on all kinds of learning opportunities, including local contacts. The Freephone number is 0800 100 900 (8am to 10pm daily) and the website address is www.learndirect.co.uk

Age Concern locally should be able to provide information. Many groups run their own learning programmes.

Age Resource will give advance information about courses, events and activities of all sorts for people aged 50 or over in different parts of England. You can contact Age Resource at the address on page 179 to find out if there is an Age Resource Desk near you.

Learning away from home

If you do not want to commit yourself to an ongoing course, short residential courses are a useful alternative, provided you can afford the fees. Intensive courses like this can be a good way of acquiring knowledge, or a skill, relatively quickly.

Residential study breaks and summer schools are offered by universities, colleges, schools and field study centres. Many people come on their own to these courses, so a study break is one solution to the problem experienced by many single people of taking a holiday on their own. Look in your newspaper for adverts or ask your travel agency.

For more information about residential study breaks, see *Time to Learn*, which is a priced booklet published twice a year by City and Guilds (address on page 181). The National Institute of Adult Continuing Education (NIACE) (address on page 184) organises Adult Learners Week every May.

Distance learning

'Distance learning' refers to learning by post, radio, television or email, or by using a distance learning package. It is one form of 'open learning': this term implies flexibility as regards the content and duration of a course; you can decide what you learn and over what period of time. All the main providers of distance learning courses have a high proportion of older students.

The Open University (address on page 185) offers courses and study packs on a vast range of subjects – such as arts, sciences, social sciences, community education and leisure – in addition to its degree course (see below).

The Open College of the Arts (address on page 185) aims to provide home-based education in a wide range of arts subjects, including music, photography, creative writing, garden design and art history. You may also be required to attend occasional tutorials at a regional study centre.

The National Extension College (NEC) (address on page 184) offers a wide variety of courses – from maths and electronics to birdwatching, counselling and business skills – including courses specifically geared to the needs of people who left school without qualifications and have not studied for some time.

In addition, colleges offering correspondence courses are widely advertised in newspapers and magazines.

 For general information on correspondence courses, or to check the credentials of a correspondence college, contact the Open and Distance Learning Quality Council (ODLQC) at the address on page 185.

Taking a degree

Most universities accept mature students for degree courses on the basis of their experience rather than the paper qualifications demanded of school-leavers. If you have not taken a degree before, you may be eligible for a grant from your local authority to cover tuition fees. Additional help with the costs of student life may be available from your local education authority.

 The Department for Education and Skills publishes a booklet called *Financial Help for Higher Education Students.* You can phone 0800 731 9133 for a copy. General information about funding and concessions for studying is available from Learndirect on Freephone 0800 100 900 (8am to 10pm daily).

The Open University (OU) has no admission qualifications, but OU students do not qualify for ordinary local authority grants. There may, however, be other help available, as explained in its booklet on financial support. An OU degree will normally take between four and six years.

 For a list of useful addresses and publications, see Age Concern Factsheet 30 *Leisure and learning.*

Community involvement

Working people often admit they really haven't a clue about what goes on in the neighbourhood they live in – which is not surprising if they leave for work early in the morning and don't return home until the evening. Becoming more involved in the life of the local community can be extremely rewarding; it can also greatly ease the transition from full-time work to retirement.

Joining a club or society

If you are interested in joining a club locally, the best source of information is your local library, where you will find leaflets and notices on a wide variety of clubs and societies. Before committing yourself to join, you should be able to have a look at a copy of their forthcoming programme and attend an initial meeting as a guest. This will give you an idea of the level at which the society is pitched and of what the atmosphere is like.

Joining a society or club is one way of taking a hobby or interest a bit further, and at the same time meeting people with similar interests. If you enjoy painting, photography or gardening, you could join an art society, photography club or horticultural society. For those who are keen to go back to their roots, family history societies exist all over the country. If you enjoy Scrabble, chess, or bridge, you could join a local club and even enter competitions. Try to strike a balance between your different interests and think too about what activities you will do with your partner, if you have one, and what on your own.

Clubs for older people

Large employers such as the civil service, the National Health Service and some big companies run clubs for former employees. If you are fit and active and have just retired, the idea of joining a club whose members are largely much older than you may not seem very appealing – and this is likely to be equally true of local Age Concern groups and organisations. However, it might be worth getting their newsletter; the club may have more to offer than you expect. An increasing number of local Age Concerns now offer leisure programmes. In addition, active retired people with a bit of time to spare are always needed as volunteers – to help organise activities and perhaps to visit housebound members.

Women's clubs

If the name Women's Institute (WI) conjures up for you a picture of jam-making and apple pies, you may be pleasantly surprised: their talks and discussions cover a great variety of topics, and they offer a wide range of courses, including running a small business and computer studies. The WI has branches in town and country alike, as does the Townswomen's Guild.

For information about your nearest WI, contact the National Federation of Women's Institutes at the address on page 184. For the address of your nearest Townswomen's Guild, contact the national office at the address on page 187.

Environmental groups

Many people spend the bulk of their working lives indoors and see retirement as an opportunity to redress the balance. Joining a group such as Friends of the Earth, the Ramblers' Association or the Royal Society for the Protection of Birds combines outdoor activities and a positive commitment to protecting the environment. The Ramblers, for example, go on regular walks and at the same time help to keep footpaths open and preserve people's right of access to the countryside.

The British Trust for Conservation Volunteers (BTCV) has local groups in rural and urban areas throughout the country. They teach and practice skills such as coppicing, hedging and dry stone walling. They also organise working holidays.

To find out your nearest group, contact the Ramblers' Association at the address on page 186, or BTCV at the address on page 180.

Working as a volunteer

Factfile

■ In 2000, people aged 55–65 were the most likely age group to help people once a month or more frequently.

Volunteering is something to be undertaken because you want to, and not because you feel you ought to. If you have time and energy to spare, working as a volunteer can be extremely satisfying. It can enable you to put the skills you have acquired while working to good use. Alternatively, it can give you the chance to do something completely different from your pre-retirement job, and perhaps to develop new skills and meet new people.

The opportunities for doing voluntary work are endless. You could do work for your church or for a political organisation. As already mentioned, you could help organise outings and other activities for a club or society you belong to. But you are most likely to find voluntary work with a voluntary agency, which range from national charities such as Age Concern and Oxfam and campaigning bodies such as Friends of the Earth to community groups and local action groups. You might already be involved with a group and now be able to take more on. It makes sense to take care when deciding what organisation to work for, just as you would with a paid job.

The following few examples give some idea of the range of work you can do as a volunteer. You could:

■ act as a guide or steward in a museum or stately home – the National Trust relies heavily on volunteers;
■ train to be a counsellor for organisations such as the Samaritans, Victim Support or Relate;
■ work with children and young people in a baby clinic, playgroup, youth club, scouts or guides group;
■ work with older people, helping with shopping or gardening, or perhaps assisting in a day centre or care home; or
■ work in a charity shop.

You could also consider public service work. For example:

- becoming a magistrate or local councillor;
- sitting on a tribunal, such as a Disability Appeals Tribunal or an Employment Tribunal; or
- participating in other public bodies, such as a school governing body.

When considering what would suit you, bear in mind that you have your experience of life to offer as well as the expertise you acquired at work. For example, people who have themselves suffered a bereavement may make good bereavement counsellors. Retired people are often more acceptable as counsellors and helpers to people in their own age group simply because they have shared similar experiences.

Think about what you have to offer, and look at your skills and experience – just as you would with a paid job. Think carefully too about how much time you want to commit: voluntary agencies will need you to be reliable and it is better to understate the time you want to give, at least at the beginning. Some voluntary agencies, such as the Citizens Advice Bureaux, the Samaritans and Relate, offer extensive training to their volunteers.

How to find voluntary work

If you have already been taking part in some voluntary activity, retirement may simply provide the opportunity to become more involved. If you haven't, there are various places to go for information about vacancies for volunteers in your area.

Age Resource (address on page 179) will be able to give you details of opportunities for all types of voluntary work in your area.

The local library will often have leaflets and notices from agencies seeking volunteers. Most reference libraries will have a copy of the *Voluntary Agencies Directory* (published by NCVO Publications) which lists the national offices of many voluntary agencies. A list of voluntary agencies in your area may be available from the library, the CAB, or the Council for Voluntary Service (CVS).

To find out where your nearest CVS is, contact the National Association of Councils for Voluntary Service (NACVS) at the address on page 184.

Volunteer bureaux Check in the local telephone directory to see if there is a volunteer bureau in your area or contact Volunteer Development England (address on page 188).

REACH (the Retired Executives Action Clearing House) (address on page 186) specialises in finding part-time expenses-only jobs with voluntary agencies for retired professionals and business men and women.

The Retired and Senior Volunteer Programme (RSVP) (address on page 186) is a volunteer programme for people over 50. Volunteers work together as a team on local community projects; many local communities have a RSVP organiser to coordinate activities.

The Experience Corps is a not-for-profit organisation which focuses on boosting the numbers of people over 50 who volunteer. You can contact them on Freephone 0800 106 080 or look on the website at www.experiencecorps.co.uk

 For information about volunteering overseas, see page 85.

For a free guide for people (of all ages) who want to volunteer, send an sae (33p) to the National Centre for Volunteering at the address on page 184, putting 'Timeguide' on the top left corner of the envelope.

Earning money in retirement

Factfile

■ In Spring 2000, 7.6 per cent of men aged 65 and over and 8.2 per cent of women aged 60 and over were still in employment.

Before deciding to take on any paid work, it is worth having a good look both at your financial position and at what you are going to get out of retirement. How much money will you need, both in the immediate future and in the years ahead? This should help you decide whether you want full-time or part-time work and how many hours a week you need.

You may feel you would prefer to reduce your expenditure in some way rather than give up any precious leisure time. On the other hand, developing an existing hobby or interest further could also turn out to be a good way of earning some extra money. Finding a new job may not be easy, however (you could be lucky and find something straightaway, but it is more likely that you will have to do some analysis and research first).

What could you do?

When you first ask yourself the question 'What do I have to offer?', you will probably think of the skills associated with your pre-retirement job. However, you may not want to carry on doing the same sort of job or even working in the same field. In order to answer the question properly, you need to take a far broader look at yourself and what you can do.

In addition to the skills directly related to your job, you are likely to have some more general skills, such as an ability to communicate well with other people or a good head for figures, for example. Think about what you like doing and feel you are good at – this will help you to draw up a profile of the kind of work you want. It can be a very useful exercise to make a list of all the skills you possess. To do this properly you will need to cast your mind over all the areas and stages of your life.

It could well be that the things you really like doing are the things you have been doing outside work. So ask yourself whether your hobbies have earning potential. If you enjoy decorating, for example, could you start doing it for other people? If you have a computer, could you go into desktop publishing or website design?

What about further training?

If you have identified gaps in your skills or qualifications, further training could help you to change direction if that's what you want to do. Or you may want to do some training just to improve your chances of getting a job or to improve or formalise your existing skills.

In addition to the various educational opportunities discussed on pages 54–58, you may be eligible for a government training grant under the New Deal 50 Plus if you are below State Pension age and have been signing on as unemployed for six months or more (see page 67). The Employment Service does provide courses free to unemployed people under the Work-based Learning scheme, but the upper age limit is 63.

Business Links (see page 70) offer courses and Learndirect (see page 56) has a number of Internet-based courses for people setting up businesses. Jobcentres/Jobcentre Plus offices should be able to tell you where you can find local work-based training.

If what you really want is recognition of your existing skills, you could go on a course locally and gain a professional qualification. Although National Vocational Qualifications (NVQs) are generally achieved in the workplace and based on your experience at work, it is possible to obtain one at a college, by means of work experience gained there. Another option is Accreditation of Prior Learning, where you put together a portfolio of past work experience that shows that you've already reached the level of competence required for an NVQ or other qualification. Ask at your local college or university to see if they offer this service.

Where to go for help

You may get help in thinking through the options from:

- a personal adviser at the local Jobcentre (which are being converted to provide a more comprehensive service as Jobcentre Plus offices);
- the local authority careers service – now called Connexions but in some areas aimed more at younger people;
- private companies – listed under 'careers advice' in the phone book. (These services can be very expensive, so always check to make sure that what they are offering is really what you want and try to get a recommendation first.)
- Internet sites (the Internet can also be very useful for researching potential employers); or
- books, tapes and CD-ROMs from your local library.

For more information about the general services available from your local Jobcentre, you can phone Employment Service Direct on **0845 606 0234** or visit the website at www.employmentservice.gov.uk

Working for an employer

Although some retired people feel attracted by the idea of becoming self-employed, many still prefer the greater security and more reliable income associated with working for someone else.

Working part-time The majority of people who earn money in retirement work part-time. Part-time work can be often be easier to find, but it is more variable in terms of what is offered and how well paid it is. However, part-timers do now have the same employment rights as full-timers doing comparable jobs.

Job-sharing provides a kind of halfway house between full-time and part-time work – two or more people share the hours, duties, pay and benefits of one full-time job.

Temporary or casual work can sometimes be a good way of finding a permanent job as many employers look first at those they already know.

There are temporary vacancies in almost every field. The easiest way to find it is through an employment agency.

Teleworking You can work at home for an employer, keeping in touch with employer and customers through computers, telephones and faxes (many teleworkers are self-employed). Teleworking is flexible and thus useful if you have caring responsibilities, for example, but can be quite isolating.

Where to look for a job

Jobcentres/Jobcentre Plus offices where, if you are under State Pension age, a personal adviser will discuss the kind of work you want and help you draw up a Jobseeker's Agreement that will be reviewed regularly (see pages 9–10 for information about Jobseeker's Allowance).

The New Deal 50 Plus is part of the general government training and employment initiative called the New Deal. It gives job-finding help to people over 50 who have been unemployed for six months or more. It used to include an Employment Credit but this has now been replaced by the 50 plus element of the Working Tax Credit (see page 24).

For more information, ask at the local Jobcentre/Jobcentre Plus (www.job-centreplus.gov.uk) or look on the website at www.newdeal.gov.uk/english/ fiftyplus/ Age Concern has a leaflet on the New Deal 50 Plus, which is available from the Information Line at the address on page 204.

Employment agencies It is worth registering with appropriate agencies because many employers approach agencies before they advertise jobs. Also, the agencies may have other resources to help you. Apart from the many ordinary employment agencies listed in the *Yellow Pages*, there are a number that specialise in finding jobs for retired older people. Some local Age Concern groups have established their own employment agencies. There are also several agencies that specialise in recruiting staff for charities.

For the names and addresses of employment agencies for older people, and of other useful organisations, see Age Concern Factsheet 31 *Older workers.*

National and local media Some national newspapers advertise different categories of job on different days of the week. It may also be worth looking in professional and trade journals. Some local radio stations advertise job vacancies and the Internet can also be useful, especially for larger employers.

Networks 'Networking' refers to making use of all the contacts that you have to obtain advice, information and jobs. Clubs and professional associations are examples of networks, but your networks will also include your family, neighbours, friends and former colleagues, and people you meet through your place of worship, a trade union or your local pub for example. Let people know that you are looking for work and ask them to let others know.

Self-advertising Putting an advertisement in the local press or a notice in a shop window or employment agency are forms of self-advertising. If you are thinking of writing to prospective employers telling them what you can offer, be sure to target effectively.

Combating ageism

You may find that some employers hold negative misconceptions about the potential of older people. Will you be in poor health? Will you be able to retrain? Will it be worth offering training if you are unlikely to continue working for long? Will you be willing to work under a less experienced, and perhaps less qualified, supervisor? These are some of the questions employers may ask if you are over 50.

Unfortunately, it is still legal to discriminate against someone on the grounds of age. However, the Government is planning to introduce legislation on age discrimination in employment to be effective from 2006. In the meantime there is only a voluntary code of practice.

Attitudes are slowly changing, however: many large employers are realising the benefits of employing older workers and making it a priority to recruit more people over 50. Nevertheless, negative stereotypes still exist and you may encounter ageism. If you want to get a job, you may need to point out the falsity of such views and to emphasise the positive aspects of age, such as experience, reliability and proven ability, and availability and flexibility.

If you are an employee and you feel that you are being unfairly treated with regard to promotion or training, speak to your human resources department or trade union or the local ACAS office (the address will be in the phone book or ask your local library).

The Third Age Employment Network (TAEN) is a national network and campaigning organisation working for better opportunities for older people to continue in training, work and self-employment – see address on page 187.

Applying for a job

When you see a suitable job vacancy, ask for an application form straight-away to allow yourself as much time as possible to fill in the form and to research the employer.

Some companies want the application to be in the form of a curriculum vitae (CV). This is a document explaining your experience at work (and in your spare time if appropriate to the vacancy) as well as your education and qualifications.

If possible, prepare your CV in advance of any vacancies and then alter it to emphasise and link your experience to that required by the advert. It should be brief (preferably not more than two sides of A4 paper) and positive. Its aim is to present you as someone worth interviewing.

The Employment Service, or an employment agency that you have regis-tered with, may be able to help you with your CV. Be wary of private firms offering this service and ask to see examples of their work before using them.

Preparing for an interview

It may be many years since you were last interviewed for a job. Preparation consists mainly of gathering background information about your prospective employer and thinking about questions you might be asked. Make a list of the points you want to bring out and ensure that you do, even if the interviewer doesn't ask you directly about them.

The Age Concern publication *Changing Direction* (see page 199) explains in detail about preparing a CV, choosing referees and writing a covering letter, as well as preparing for an interview.

Working for yourself

'Setting up your own business' can encompass anything from doing some dressmaking or decorating for friends and neighbours to running a shop or working as a management consultant. An increasing number of people are becoming self-employed. However, the failure rate is high for those setting up in business on their own and you will need to be well-organised and be prepared to put in a lot of hard work. You can reduce the risks you take through research and planning before you commit yourself.

A new business should set clear goals and have a business plan. The network of Business Link operators in England offers advice and services to those setting up new businesses and can help with research and business plans. They can offer guidance on:

- assessing your current skills;
- choosing your business type;
- planning and researching your business idea;
- financing your business; and
- untangling the legal aspects of a new business.

To find the address of your nearest Business Link, contact the national office at the address on page 180.

Business Link suggests that some of the questions you should ask yourself include:

- Who and where are your potential customers?
- How much will it cost to produce/provide your goods or services?
- What should you charge your customers?
- Will you need any suppliers?
- Will you need to comply with any regulations?

Offering a service

Offering some sort of service on a freelance basis can be an ideal way of continuing to earn some money when you have retired. If you enjoyed your pre-retirement job, you might like to carry on doing the same sort of work. Alternatively you might prefer to develop a hobby or leisure interest into a money-making activity.

Consultancy

It may be possible to set yourself up as a consultant in a field that you know and have contacts in, whether it be fashion, computers, tax, or even retirement for example. You will need to make sure that you keep up to date with developments in your area and it may be worth seeking professional advice from those already working in the field.

Buying an existing business

You can find out about the availability of the businesses that interest you through the appropriate trade journals or a business transfer agency (look in your local *Yellow Pages*).

Once you have found a business that seems suitable, you should try to discover as much as you can about it. Ask as many questions as you need and get the answers in writing. Apart from anything else you will want to find out what the location is like, what reputation the business has in the area, and why the present owners want to sell.

When you get to the stage of serious negotiation, it is wise to seek professional help – an accountant, solicitor, and a surveyor if it involves property.

Starting from scratch

One advantage of starting a business from scratch is that you will not run the risk of being taken in by someone trying to dispose of a business for dubious reasons. You may also need less capital because you will not have to pay for intangible assets such as goodwill. An obvious disadvantage, especially for an older person, is that it may take some time for the business to become viable. In general, the more personalised the product or service you are selling, the more likely it is that you will decide to start from scratch.

Whatever your idea, you need to ask yourself whether you have the necessary skills – such as research, marketing, selling, book-keeping, planning, dealing with people – as well as the stamina and the capital. Will you be able to cope with the insecurity and the hard work? Talk to people in the field, look at books and websites or go on a course. Your local Business Link and the relevant trade and professional organisations may be able to supply information and contacts.

Buying a franchise

A growing number of franchises are available. A franchise is the grant of a licence by one person (the franchiser) to another (the franchisee) which entitles the franchisee to trade under the franchiser's name. The franchise also receives help with establishing and running the business. Franchises on offer in the UK include such household names as the Body Shop, Clark's Shoes and Burger King, as well as many smaller, recently established ones.

One advantage of a franchise is that you take fewer risks and are likely to have fewer start-up problems. The disadvantage is that you need a significant amount of capital to buy a franchise as the initial fee can be very large, on top of what you have to pay for premises, equipment, stock, etc. You also have to pay royalties to the franchiser. You should check all the details just as if you were buying the business from someone else.

An explanatory guide, *The ethics of franchising*, is available from the British Franchise Association (BFA) at the address on page 180. The BFA also publishes a code of practice.

Tax and self-employment

If you work for yourself you should be treated as self-employed for tax purposes. However, if you contract out your services to one client at a time, you may be treated as if you were employed. To be properly self-employed you normally need several clients and to work mainly on your own premises. In that case, you will be dealt with under self-assessment (see page 29) and have to work out your own profits and pay your own Income Tax. If you are under State Pension age, you may also have to pay your own National Insurance contributions.

If you become self-employed, you are now legally obliged to notify the Inland Revenue when you start. You can write a letter to your local tax office or you can obtain Inland Revenue leaflet P/SE/1, *Thinking of working for yourself*, and fill in form CWF1 which it contains.

For more information about tax for self-employed people, see the Age Concern publication *Your Taxes and Savings* (see page 198).

Travel

In retirement you may have less disposable income than when you were at work, but you also have more time. This should mean that you are able to get about more cheaply – and usually more pleasantly – by travelling at off-peak times and taking advantage of travel bargains. Considerable fare reductions are also available to older people on a number of different types of transport.

Concessionary travel

Local buses

In England, there is a national minimum bus concession scheme. While some local authorities may offer better concessions, all authorities must offer a minimum concession of half fare, for travel after 9.30am, for all people of State Pension age (although in April 2003 men may be able to qualify for the concession at the age of 60). Apply to your local authority for details in your area. Travel is limited to within the issuing local authority but some local neighbouring authorities have joint arrangements.

In Scotland, pensioners have been entitled to free off-peak bus travel since October 2002. Ages are expected to be equalised at 60 by April 2003. In Wales, all pensioners have had free local bus travel within their own authority since April 2002, with ages likely to be equalised at 60 in April 2003.

Trains

All rail companies give one-third reductions on most types of ticket to people who have a Senior Railcard. This costs £18 (in 2002) and is valid for one year. It is available to people aged 60 or over, provided that proof of age is given.

Senior Railcard users can also buy a Rail Senior Card for £12 (in 2002), for savings of up to 25 per cent on cross border rail travel in Europe.

For further details and an application form, see the leaflet *Senior Railcard*, which is available from most stations and rail-appointed travel agents.

The Disabled Persons Railcard, which costs £14 (in 2002), offers similar discounts to the Senior Railcard but gives you the option of taking a companion with you at the same reduced rate.

Coaches

National Express offers up to 30 per cent off many standard fares for holders of the Advantage50 Discount Coach Card. This costs £9 a year (in 2002) and is available to anyone aged 50 and over. A three-year card that costs £19 is also available. Other coach operators may also offer concessions but may have different age limits.

For most services you will need to book in advance. As with trains, travelling on Friday (and on Saturday in July and August) is more expensive. It is always worth keeping an eye open for special offers.

If you are considering travelling by coach, it is worth checking where the pick-up points are. You will not necessarily have to start or end your journey at a coach station.

 For more information, call National Express on 08705 80 80 80 or look at the website at www.gobycoach.com

Air

Some airlines do offer reduced rates for older people on both domestic and international flights, but these may not be on the cheapest fares available.

The cheapest fares are usually the ones with the most restrictions and need to be booked well in advance. A number of conditions often apply to these fares, such as that they are only available on certain days of the week or times of the year, and there is a minimum and maximum length of stay. Cheap tickets are often bought through so-called 'bucket shops', which buy them in bulk from the airlines. It is also worth looking for advertisements in national and local papers and on the Internet.

Sea

Some ferry operators offer discounts to Senior Railcard holders, and others offer concessions to passengers above a certain age.

Travelling for fun

If you have time to spare, it can be enjoyable to travel around for its own sake rather than simply as a means of getting from one place to another. If you haven't got a car, you could try one of the various rover tickets on offer.

Rover tickets can be bought from most major bus companies in the provinces. They give you unlimited travel for a day in their area. One-day travel passes will give you unlimited travel within London.

Tourist trail passes are available from National Express. They give you unlimited travel for different periods – for example for five days' travel within a ten day period – with extra discounts for Discount Card holders.

Coach trips Days out to sporting events, stately homes and so on are organised by many coach companies, which also provide group travel for clubs and societies of all kinds.

Community minibuses exist in many areas, run by community transport groups for other voluntary organisations. They do not usually put on transport for individuals, but a group of older people getting together for an outing should be able to hire a minibus quite cheaply.

 To find out about community transport groups in your area, contact the Community Transport Association at the address on page 181.

Travel for people with disabilities

Buses

The Government has required all new buses introduced after January 2000 to be accessible. However, it will be some years before all vehicles in service will comply. As well as offering wheelchair access, they will have low steps, easy to grip handrails and easy to push bells.

Trains

Many mainline railway stations are accessible, but facilities and availability of staff vary widely. Many smaller stations are unstaffed. Facilities on trains also vary widely. In older trains people in wheelchairs may have to travel in the guard's van and the toilets will probably not be wheelchair accessible.

To find out what facilities are available on a particular journey, you should phone the train operator before you travel. They can advise you on the most suitable trains and stations to use, and provide assistance at the departure and arrival stations.

All the train companies and Railtrack have adopted a code of practice to offer people with disabilities a universal common standard of service. The code applies to people who have advised of their travel arrangements in advance and who are either wheelchair bound, blind or partially sighted, or deaf and disabled and holders of a Disabled Persons Railcard.

Generally, train companies can guarantee assistance if at least 24 hours notice is given, although at small stations, for example, 48 hours notice may be necessary. To find out which train company to contact, telephone the National Rail Enquiry Service on 0845 748 4950.

The leaflet *Rail travel for disabled passengers*, which is available free from main railway stations, gives advice and contact addresses.

Coaches

Again, facilities for disabled people vary widely, so check with the coach company about facilities at both ends of the journey and on the coach.

The Government has required that all new large coaches be wheelchair accessible from January 2005, but it will be many years before they all are. Existing coaches cannot usually carry wheelchair passengers. Many coach operators will provide assistance for disabled people, but seven days notice is usually required.

Air and sea

Air transport has become much easier for people with disabilities; however, it is always wise to phone the airline or airport first to check what facilities are available and whether any special arrangements need to be made. The same is true if you are travelling by sea.

There is a website (www.everybody.co.uk) with information on the services offered to people with disabilities by 50 major airlines. It also lists hotels in the UK that are accessible.

Door-to-door transport

If you are disabled and cannot use ordinary public transport, and do not have access to a car, there are a number of door-to-door transport schemes you may be able to use. Charges are usually much lower than for an ordinary taxi service.

Social cars With these schemes people volunteer to use their own cars to drive people who cannot use public transport. Drivers receive expenses, and you contribute a non-profit fare – usually more than a bus fare but less than for a taxi. Ask at your local library or Citizens Advice Bureau (CAB) about schemes in your area. Schemes are often run by the local Volunteer Bureau, Council for Voluntary Service (CVS) or Rural Community Council. Some are run by the British Red Cross or the Women's Royal Voluntary Service (WRVS).

Dial-a-rides These schemes use converted cars or minibuses with tail-lifts or ramps. Schemes exist all over the country under a variety of names; some will take you anywhere within their area, while others concentrate on a few selected destinations. Most will only take you on local trips and they will not take you on journeys for which local authority or health transport is available. Most schemes want you to register with them and to book your journey in advance. Some charge will be made. Ask at the local library or CAB for details of local schemes, or try the local authority transport planning department or social services department.

Taxicard schemes These enable disabled people living in most London boroughs to use taxis at greatly reduced fares. Contact your local council to see if it runs such a scheme.

Cars

For many people with disabilities a car is the only suitable form of transport, and having a car greatly increases their independence. If you are thinking of buying a car, both the Mobility Advice and Vehicle Information Service (MAVIS) and the Mobility Information Service (MIS) offer information and advice to disabled drivers.

For more information, contact MAVIS or MIS at the addresses on page 183. The Research Institute for Consumer Affairs publishes guides for older and disabled car users, including *The ins and outs of choosing a car*. For more information, contact RICA at the address on page 186.

Driving licences There is no age limit for driving a car, but if you have or develop a disability or medical condition that could affect your driving, you must by law notify the Driving Vehicle Licensing Agency (DVLA). The list of notifiable medical conditions is in its leaflet *What you need to know about driving licences*, which is available from post offices.

However, when you reach 70, you have to renew your licence and every three years after that. The renewal form will be sent to you automatically by the DVLA. It requires that you declare whether you suffer from any of the notifiable medical conditions. If you do suffer from any of these, you may be required to have a medical examination or take a driving test.

Motability If you get the higher mobility component of the Disability Living Allowance (see page 26), the Motability scheme may allow you to put your benefit towards the cost of leasing a new car or buying a new or used car, wheelchair or scooter on hire purchase.

For more information, contact Motability at the address on page 183.

Insurance Some companies offer much better deals for drivers aged over 50. Age Concern Insurance Services is one company that offers good rates for older and disabled people. Some companies may have special restrictions, or require medical examinations each year when the contract is due for renewal, so check the wording of the policy carefully. Always shop around before taking out insurance.

VAT and car tax People with disabilities may be exempt from car tax and from VAT on adaptations, repairs and maintenance. For further information contact RADAR at the address on page 185.

Parking The Blue Badge Scheme (formerly known as the Orange Badge Scheme) provides a national system of parking concessions for some disabled people travelling either as drivers or passengers. Badge-holders are exempt from certain parking restrictions, including that they can park free at parking meters and for up to three hours on single and double yellow lines. Certain London borough run their own schemes.

A leaflet giving full details of the scheme can be obtained from the Mobility and Inclusion Unit of the Department of Transport, Local Government and the Regions at the address on page 181.

Access guides Most major towns and cities public access guides. These list local shops, theatres, restaurants and other amenities, and indicate how easy they are to use. RADAR can tell you how to get hold of these guides and also has its own publications on access and mobility.

Tripscope

Tripscope gives free telephone information and advice on travel and transport for older and disabled people (see address on page 187). It is not a travel agency but it will help you plan a particular journey.

For more about transport for people with disabilities, including many useful addresses and publications, see Age Concern Factsheet 26 *Travel information for older people.*

Going on holiday

For most people holidays are limited to two or three weeks a year – and for those with school-age children holidays usually have to be taken during the school holidays. Once you are retired, you have several great advantages: you have the freedom and flexibility to travel at off-peak times; you can go away more often, if you can afford it; and you can stay away for longer. You may also have different priorities: change and stimulus may now be what you are looking for, rather than rest and relaxation.

Holiday ideas
Activity holidays

When they are working, many people go on holiday looking for a relaxing break. In retirement you may be looking for something a bit more stimulating than just sitting on the beach. Activity holidays have a special appeal; the following ideas are just some of the possibilities:

Special interest holidays There are many operators running special interest holidays. Details can be found in specialist magazines or from the National Tourist Boards, tourist information centres and travel agents. These holidays cover many areas, including for example arts and crafts, sport, outdoor pursuits, history, cooking, bridge, music and languages. The Pre-Retirement Association (address on page 185) offers retirement planning holidays at several locations in the UK.

Working holidays are another possibility. The British Trust for Conservation Volunteers (address on page 180) is one example of an organisation which runs working holidays.

Town twinning exchanges with the European counterpart town are organised by many local groups. If your town has a European twin, you could ask the local council for information about related activities.

Cycling holidays are a wonderful way to see the countryside. Careful planning using large-scale maps will ensure that you see the best country, avoid the steepest hills and have somewhere to stay at night.

The Cyclists' Touring Club (address on page 181) can provide information about cycling in other countries as well as the UK and offers an extensive range of tours.

Walking holidays are another good way to see the countryside. The Ramblers' Association offers walking holidays both in this country and abroad. All holidays are carefully graded, ranging from easier short walks to tough mountain walking.

For more information, contact the Ramblers' Association at the address on page 186.

Reunion holidays If you have relatives abroad and are thinking of a reunion visit, it might be worth joining a 'friendship club'. Lion World Travel, for example, has four long-standing clubs. Membership entitles you to newsletters and discount flights.

For more information, contact Lion World Travel Ltd at the address on page 182.

Specialist operators

Many ordinary holiday companies offer special holidays for older people. Local travel agents will advise about particular holidays. Two examples are Cosmos, which runs 'Golden Times' holidays for the over-55s, and Portland, which has a 'Young at Heart' brochure.

Saga is one company that provides holidays exclusively for the over-50s, including many special interest holidays. Some local Age Concern organisations and groups run their own holidays, usually for more active older people.

Taking a holiday through one of these operators can mean competitive prices as they are able to take advantage of out-of-season and party rates.

Many are also able to offer couriers who are trained to look after the needs of older travellers.

 For information about their over-50s holidays, contact Saga Holidays Ltd at the address on page 186.

Holidays for single people

Holidays can pose particular problems for people on their own. The greatest is obviously lack of a companion, but there is also the considerable extra expense of the single room supplements which are charged by some companies.

One way round the problem of holidaying on your own is to go on an activity holiday, such as those suggested above. This ensures that you will be doing something you enjoy and that you will meet other people with similar interests.

But this is no solution if what you enjoy is travelling around at your own pace, sightseeing and soaking up the local atmosphere. You might well find a companion through one of the friendship clubs, or you may wish to contact the Single Travellers Action Group (STAG). Members receive newsletters giving details of hotels and supplement-free holidays in the UK and abroad.

 For more information, contact STAG at the address on page 187.

Long-stay holidays

Long-stay holidays are best taken when the rest of the world is at work. April, May, September and October are good months for long-stay holiday-makers; roads, ferries and airports are less busy than at peak times, accommodation is cheaper and less booked up, yet it is warm enough for outdoor activities such as cycling, walking, camping and caravanning. You can check on local weather conditions with the national tourist office. Some special long-stay winter holidays are available, often at very cheap rates.

Long-stay packages

If while working you have normally chosen package holidays, then a long-stay package may be the best option for your first long-stay holiday. It may also be a good first step if you are considering moving abroad on a more permanent basis, as discussed on pages 103–106.

Some package holidays offer a substantial programme of daytime activities and excursions and evening entertainment. People who opt for a self-catering apartment rather than hotel accommodation are unlikely to have the same range of entertainment provided.

You could take your car and rent a cottage or farmhouse in a village or right out in the country. Many companies offer complete packages including rented accommodation and travel.

Arranging your own holiday

The joy of arranging your own holiday is that you can plan it entirely to suit yourself. For example, you may want to stay in the old part of an interesting and well-placed town or city, but if you look through the holiday brochures, you will find that most rented properties are on the coast or in rural areas.

Finding your own accommodation to rent is best done on the spot but in advance of a long stay. One good way to do this is to go on a short package holiday to the area you are thinking of staying in. If you are a car driver, you could explore an area on the way to another destination. A good place to start is the local tourist information office, which should be able to give you a list of rented properties in the area.

Home swapping

If you like the idea of a long-stay holiday but can't really afford it, home swapping might be a solution. You live in someone else's home for an agreed period of time, while they live in yours.

When you have fixed up a swap, it is vital to make certain practical arrangements:

■ Sort out who pays gas, electricity and phone bills, and the position with food in the freezer.

■ Check with your insurance company the position regarding house contents while visitors are living in the house.

■ Leave simple instructions for domestic appliances, basic information about local bus and train services, and emergency phone numbers for a doctor, plumber and electrician.

■ Arrange for a neighbour to drop in and make sure all is well and to be 'on call' in case of problems.

You can save further money by agreeing to exchange cars as well, subject to satisfactory insurance arrangements.

If you are interested in home swapping, one agency that arranges home swaps is Intervac (address on page 182).

Voluntary work abroad

Another cheap way of having a long-stay holiday is to work abroad as a volunteer.

The British Executive Service Overseas (BESO) needs people with management, professional or technical skills for short assignments of two or three months' duration. BESO pays the cost of air travel and insurance, while accommodation and subsistence are usually provided by the organisation requesting assistance. Voluntary Services Overseas (VSO) takes volunteers up to the age of 70.

If you are interested in voluntary work abroad, contact BESO or VSO at the addresses on page 180 and 188.

Camping and caravanning

Camping and caravanning offer great flexibility and freedom of movement and work out a lot cheaper than holidays that involve hotel accommodation or house rental – once you have invested in the basic equipment.

If you have never tried this kind of holiday before, it is a good idea to try out a short package holiday first, with a company such as Eurocamp or Canvas Holidays. They have fully equipped luxury tents and mobile homes in sites all over Europe. Many companies offer three weeks for the price of two out of season.

A motorised caravan can be a good option for older people as it does away with the whole business of towing, hitching and unhitching. You could try hiring caravan and equipment to begin with.

If your trial run is a success, you might consider joining the Camping and Caravanning Club (CCC). Its monthly magazine has many helpful articles as well as advertisements for new and second-hand caravans and equipment.

For more information, contact the CCC at the address on page 181.

Planning your holiday
Protection for travellers

For your own peace of mind, it is worth making sure that the holiday firm you use is a member of the Association of British Travel Agents (ABTA). This means that their booking conditions will conform to ABTA's code of conduct, and if the firm closes down ABTA will help you get your money back. There is also an arbitration scheme to deal with complaints about members.

If you have a complaint about a member firm, contact ABTA at the address on page 180.

Passport and visas

If your passport needs renewing, make sure you allow plenty of time for delays at the Passport Office.

Check with the tour operator or embassy whether you will need a visa. Visas may be needed for stays over a certain length.

Health care abroad

Immunisation Check with the appropriate embassy or your own doctor whether you need any vaccinations (your GP is entitled to charge you for this service). Social security leaflet T6 *Health advice for travellers* gives information for people travelling overseas. You can get a copy from your local social security office or by phoning the Health Literature Line on Freephone 0800 555 777.

Medical treatment You are covered by the NHS only while you are in the UK. The full cost of medical services abroad has to be paid unless there are reciprocal agreements. In European Union countries you are entitled to treatment on a similar basis to the national population (which is not necessarily free). To ensure that you receive this, you must apply for form E111 before you go away. You can get this, free of charge, from a post office, on production of your passport. Leaflet T6 *Health advice for travellers* (see above) gives details of what you pay for and what is free.

Insurance

Holiday insurance should be taken out at the time the holiday is booked because most companies give some cover in the event of cancellation. It can be harder to get insurance as you get older as some insurers impose terms or restrict cover for those over 70. Shop around a range of insurers to get the best deal as it could save you money and ensure that you get the cover you need. Look at the upper limits not just for medical treatment but for possessions and personal money. Look too at any additional services the policy offers – does it, for example, cover repatriation costs and a 24-hour medical helpline?

A free leaflet about holiday and car insurance is available from the Association of British Insurers at the address on page 179. Advice on taking your car abroad is available from the AA or RAC.

Home security while you are away

Ideally, you want to give the impression that your house is still occupied – an obviously empty house is an invitation to burglars. The well-known give-away clues that indicate an absent owner are uncut grass and free newspapers or junk mail stuck in a letterbox or lying in the porch. If you defrost the fridge or freezer, don't leave the door wide open – instead, stick a wedge of paper in to stop the door closing.

There is no substitute for getting someone to keep an eye on the place for you, and if possible switching lights on and off, drawing curtains and so on. You might even consider paying someone a nominal caretaking allowance.

Always tell the insurance company which covers your property and contents that you are going to be away for more than a couple of weeks. It may insist on extra security precautions if cover is to be maintained.

Paying bills

If you are going to be away for a long time, you could set up a monthly direct debit or standing order from your bank or building society account to pay for gas, electricity, phone and other bills likely to arrive in your absence. If your credit card is directly linked to your bank, you could arrange to pay your credit card bill out of funds in your current account.

State benefits

You should contact your local social security office to find out whether any benefits you receive will be affected by your absence.

For information about arrangements for payment of your State Pension while you are away, see page 8.

Road tax and car insurance

If you are leaving your car at home, you might look into getting a refund on your insurance. For a refund of road tax your car will need to be off the public highway.

Can you afford a holiday?

It may be that you simply can't afford a holiday. Although it is not possible to get financial help for holidays from social security, some social services departments make occasional grants towards holidays. The Holiday Care Service has details of national charities that have been known to give such grants. Your local Age Concern, local authority or CAB might know about local charities that could help.

 For information about all types of holiday for people with special needs, contact the Holiday Care Service at the address on page 182.

It is possible to have a change of scene by being a 'homesitter'; ie a caretaker when a family is away on holiday. Homesitters Ltd vets prospective homesitters. You must be available for at least eight weeks a year. You get travel expenses, food and a fee.

 For more information, contact Homesitters Ltd at the address on page 182.

Home swapping (see pages 84–85) and working holidays (see page 81) are other ways of having a relatively cheap holiday.

Holidays for people with disabilities

There are a number of organisations that offer help to disabled people who are planning a holiday:

The Holiday Care Service is a charity that gives free information and advice on holidays for people with disabilities. It also has a factsheet listing organisations that provide escorts for people who cannot − or do not want to − travel alone.

Local Age Concerns sometimes organise holidays specifically for frail or disabled people. If not, they may know of other agencies in the area that do.

Local authority social services departments sometimes have their own accommodation for older and disabled people.

RADAR (Royal Association for Disability and Rehabilitation) publishes holiday factsheets and books, including *Holidays in Britain and Ireland* and *Holidays and travel abroad*.

 For a list of its holiday factsheets and books, or information about respite care, contact RADAR at the address on page 185.

Charities such as Arthritis Care and the Multiple Sclerosis Society, for example, often provide information on holidays, and some have their own holiday homes or organise holidays for special groups.

Holidays for carers

If you are a carer and want a holiday break, it may be possible for a bed to be found in a hospital or local authority care home for the person you care for. Ask your GP or the local social services department.

If the person you care for wants to stay at home while you are away, the Holiday Care Service can provide information about agencies that can arrange for care in the home.

 Age Concern Factsheet 6 is called *Finding help at home*. The Alzheimer's Society has an information sheet on holidays and short-term care. It is available from the Society at the address on page 194.

Financial help may be available through social security towards the cost of short-term care for those on very low incomes.

 For more information about holidays for older and disabled people, and for carers, including the addresses of useful organisations, see Age Concern Factsheet 4 *Holidays for older people*.

Your home

Does your present home suit you? Is it likely to go on suiting you as you get older?

This chapter examines the options that are available, including retirement housing, special housing or moving abroad.

It also looks at what you can do to make life easier if you want to stay living where you are, including improving home security and getting repairs and improvements done, and at how to use the value of your home to increase your income.

- Moving house
- Home security
- Repairs and improvements
- Raising income or capital from your home

Moving house

Factfile

In England in 2000–2001:

- 57 per cent of owner-occupiers without a mortgage were 65 and over.

- 63 per cent of owner-occupiers without a mortgage were retired.

- 3 per cent of owner-occupiers with a mortgage were 65 and over.

- 35 per cent of those renting from local authorities were 65 and over.

Many people see retirement as the signal to sell the family home and move somewhere smaller. If you don't think it is likely to continue to suit you as you grow older, you may well decide to move now. Most retired people move into another ordinary house, but some may like the idea of moving into housing specially designed for older people. This section looks at the housing options, including those open to tenants and people with limited capital who have fewer choices than those with more capital.

Points to consider

If you are considering whether you should move house, here are some questions you might ask yourself:

- Do you like the area, and is it likely to change in the near future?
- Are you near relatives and friends?
- Are you near shops, public transport and other amenities?
- Is your home expensive to run – in particular, to heat?
- Is it easy to clean and maintain?
- Is it larger than you need? (Remember, however, that you are likely to be spending more time in it now.)

- Is it in need of repair or likely to need major repairs in the next few years?

Don't underestimate the cost of moving house. With agent's fees and removal costs (and Stamp Duty for property over £60,000), it could be as much as 10 per cent of the value of your new home.

If you do decide to move, you will obviously need to look at your proposed new home just as critically as you looked at your old one. It might also be worth looking much further ahead: for example, would it be possible to put in a bathroom downstairs if someone in the family began to find the stairs difficult? A house with very steep stairs might not be a good choice.

If you are thinking of moving to a new area, the following points might also be worth considering:

- If you are moving to be nearer relatives, such as your children for example, you may not know many other people in the new area and may end up missing the friends you now have. Your children could themselves move away from the area in the future.
- If you are a couple and one of you dies, will the other still want to live in that area?
- Is the area noisy in the daytime (you are likely to be at home much more than previously)?
- Is the area as convenient as where you live at present in terms of shops, transport, doctor, library, pub, etc?
- Is the outside of the house and surrounding area well lit at night? Would you feel secure there?

You can research the move – if you want to move to the seaside, for example, it may be worth spending a week in the area during the winter months and again in the peak holiday season before making the move.

Moving to retirement housing

You may decide to move to retirement housing for a variety of reasons – you would like accommodation that is smaller or more manageable or you feel that the presence of a warden would give you peace of mind, for example. However, think about whether you could receive some of the extra security or support services in your existing home (see 'Staying put' section below).

Think carefully too about how you would feel living in accommodation which may be smaller than your present home, perhaps in an unfamiliar area, and which is occupied exclusively by older people. Although you will probably want to discuss your options with friends and family, make sure that you make the final decision.

Specially designed housing without a scheme manager

Many local authorities and housing associations have housing for rent that is either purpose-built or converted specially for older people, but without the support of a warden or scheme manager, and many private companies sell similar housing.

Such schemes are usually within easy reach of shops, public transport and other services, and in a relatively flat area. Special design features might include level or ramped access, wide doorways, waist-high sockets and switches, and a walk-in shower with a seat.

If you are thinking of buying a home that is said to be specially designed for older people, make sure that it does have most of these features. Some housing that is marketed as being designed for older people is in fact barely different from ordinary housing.

 For more information on rented retirement housing, see Age Concern Factsheet 8 *Moving into rented housing.*

Retirement housing with a scheme manager

Retirement or sheltered housing for rent is provided mainly by local councils and housing associations. You can also buy retirement housing (usually on a leasehold basis), both from private companies and from housing associations.

Retirement housing schemes usually consist of a number of self-contained one-or-two-bedroom flats or sometimes bungalows, usually with a resident warden or manager and an alarm system in each home for emergency use. Both tenants and owner-occupiers pay a service charge for the cost of the scheme manager and other services.

Retirement housing schemes sometimes have communal facilities such as a shared lounge or laundry. Some have a guest bedroom which can be rented out if family or friends want to visit you.

Many schemes have a warden – nowadays more often known by a different title such as 'scheme manager', 'resident manager' or 'house manager'. The manager normally lives on the site. Their role varies, so find out how much of the day they are on duty as 24-hour cover is rare. Generally, managers can call for help in an emergency, report repair problems and keep a neighbourly eye on residents. They will not normally carry out personal services such as shopping, cooking, cleaning or nursing.

Types of housing that provide a greater degree of support are discussed on pages 101–103.

Buying retirement housing

Many developers (and some local authorities and housing associations) sell sheltered housing for older people. Once all the properties in a scheme have been sold, the developer usually hands the scheme over to a separate management organisation (sometimes a housing association), which assumes responsibility for running it. The management organisation will be responsible for services such as cleaning and maintenance of common areas.

When buying a new property, it is advisable to buy it from a builder registered with the National House Building Council (NHBC). The NHBC has a code of practice applying to all retirement housing sold after 1 April 1990.

Copies of the code of practice are available from the NHBC at the address on page 190.

If you are considering buying retirement housing, think about the following points:

- Is the area relatively flat, and is the scheme conveniently placed for public transport, shops and other services and facilities?
- Does the design of the flat include most of the features mentioned on page 93?
- What facilities are there for residents' use?
- Would you be able to fit your furniture in the flat?
- Are the builder and management organisation experienced at providing retirement housing? Do they belong to the Association of Retirement Housing Managers whose members have to follow a code of practice?
- Who runs the management organisation? If it is run jointly by the leaseholders, are you obliged under your lease to become a shareholder or can you opt out of this? What are the implications if you choose not to become a shareholder of the management organisation?
- How much is the service charge and what does it cover? What else will you have to pay for (for example ground rent)?
- If, as should be the case, there is a separate 'sinking' fund for repairs, how do residents contribute to it?
- What are the arrangements if you want to resell? Do you get back the full market value?
- What are the scheme manager's main duties and what are the arrangements when he or she is off duty?
- Does the lease cover what happens if your health deteriorates?
- Who owns the freehold on the property?
- If the freehold is owned by the management organisation, what are the arrangements if you and the other leaseholders wish to buy it?

Many of your basic rights as a leaseholder are covered by the law. Some rights, however, will depend on what is included in the lease which you sign. Seek professional advice before you sign anything.

For more information about buying retirement housing, see Age Concern Factsheet 2 *Retirement housing for sale*. It includes a list of some of the private agencies which specialise in marketing retirement housing. See also the Age Concern Books publication *A Buyer's Guide to Retirement Housing* (details on page 200).

Advice for people living in retirement housing is available from AIMS (Advice Information and Mediation Service for retirement housing) at the address on page 188. AIMS publishes, in conjunction with LEASE (The Leasehold Advisory Service), a free booklet called *Leasehold retirement housing: your rights and remedies*.

Options for people with limited capital

Most retirement housing is sold at full market value and you get back the full value when you resell. If you live in a flat or in housing which is not in very good condition, you may find that after selling up you cannot afford to buy another home outright. This may also apply if you want to move to a more expensive area. If you are in this position, your options may be rather limited, but in some areas there may be other options.

Shared ownership Some councils and housing associations run schemes where you can part buy and part rent sheltered housing. You buy a proportion of the property's value – normally 25, 50 or 75 per cent. You will generally have to pay rent on the remainder as well as the service charge. If you leave the scheme you receive your share of the property's value at the time of leaving.

Leasehold Schemes for the Elderly (LSE) These schemes, run by a small number of housing associations, allow you to buy a 70 per cent share of the lease, with the remaining share owned by the housing association. You receive 70 per cent of the property's value when you sell. No new LSE schemes are being built, but some LSE properties may be available as resales.

To find out if there is a shared ownership or LSE scheme in your area, contact your local council or housing association or the Elderly Accommodation Counsel at the address on page 189.

Interest-only mortgages Some older people may be able to get an interest-only mortgage from a building society (see page 119). You pay the interest each month, but the capital is not repaid until you die or the property is eventually sold. A number of lenders may consider giving these loans, but policies vary, so shop around locally.

Moving to rented accommodation

If you want to move house and cannot afford to buy what you want, you may consider moving into rented accommodation. The main sources of rented accommodation are local authorities and housing associations.

Your local authority, housing advice centre, CAB, local Age Concern or the Elderly Accommodation Counsel (address on page 189) should be able to give you information about rented housing in your area.

For more information on renting from local authorities and housing associations, see Age Concern Factsheet 8 *Moving into rented housing*.

Private rented accommodation

Moving into private rented accommodation is less likely to be a good choice for most older people, largely because of anxieties about rent levels and security of tenure. All new tenancies in the private sector are now let on an assured shorthold basis. This means that the landlord will have the right to bring your tenancy to an end after the first six months. Always get advice before signing a tenancy agreement with a private landlord.

For more information, see Age Concern Factsheet 36 *Private tenants' rights.*

Council and housing association rented accommodation

Many councils and housing associations have very long waiting lists. Some will not give priority to homeowners for rehousing in rented accommodation and most are unable to give priority to people who are returning from living abroad. If you wish to apply for housing in a different area, you may find that the council or housing association will not consider applicants from outside the area.

If you become a housing association tenant, you will usually be given an 'assured tenancy', unlike people who became tenants before 1 January 1989, and council tenants, who will be 'secure' tenants'. This means that you will have more limited protection against unreasonable rent increases. Assured tenants nevertheless have considerable rights and cannot normally be asked to leave unless they fail to keep to the tenancy conditions.

For more information, see Age Concern Factsheet 35 *Rights for council and housing association tenants.*

Options for existing tenants
Exchanges

If you are already a council or housing association tenant and you want to move within your area, you can ask for a transfer, but this could take some time. If you have a medical or other urgent need to move, you should be given priority for a transfer. Most councils and housing associations allow tenants to exchange with each other, but this obviously depends on someone else wanting to live in your home.

If you want to move to another area, the council or housing association may have 'reciprocal' arrangements to rehouse a certain number of applicants from another area. A very small number of people achieve a move through the HOMES Mobility Scheme which enables people to move to be near relatives or for other strong social reasons; contact your local council or housing association for details.

Any council or housing association tenant can attempt to swap homes with another on their own initiative through the Homeswap scheme, which is a UK-wide register of tenants who want to swap homes.

 A leaflet called *Homeswaps: an easy way to move* should be available from your local authority housing department, housing advice centre or CAB.

Right to buy

Council tenants If you have been a council tenant for at least two years, you will usually have the right to buy your home from the council. You are not, however, entitled to buy your home if you live in sheltered housing. If you have the right to buy your home, you will be entitled to a discount on the market price based on how long you have lived in your home. If you sell it within three years, you may have to repay some of this discount.

Housing association tenants Housing association assured tenants do not have the right to buy except in limited circumstances, although your housing association may choose to offer its tenants the right to buy their home.

Tenants' Incentive Scheme

If you are a housing association tenant, you may also be able to get a grant under the Tenants' Incentive Scheme to enable you to move out of your home and buy another property privately. Ask your housing association for details.

Buying a freehold

If you live in a leasehold flat, you may have the right to join with other leaseholders and collectively buy the freehold, under the Housing and

Urban Development Act 1993. This option can be a positive one for lease-holders who are not happy with the management service received from the freeholder.

The Commonhold and Leasehold Reform Act 2002 also makes it easier for leaseholders to buy collectively the freehold of their block by reducing the percentage of those needing to take part from two-thirds to half of all leaseholders. The Act also introduces a new form of tenure called 'commonhold' which should provide a more effective system for the future ownership and management of blocks of flats.

Buying a freehold would be particularly advantageous for anyone who has a short lease, which is otherwise a diminishing asset. Be aware also that you may have the right to extend the lease.

For more information, see Age Concern Factsheet 2 *Retirement housing for sale* or the government leaflet *Leasehold flats*. Copies are available from councils, housing advice centres or the Office of the Deputy Prime Minister (ODPM) at the address on page 190. For more information on leasehold legislation, contact AIMS at the address on page 188.

Moving to special housing

People who find it difficult to manage on their own may prefer to move to some sort of special housing. There are various types of special housing available to suit different needs. These include:

- housing specially designed for older people, but without a warden (see page 94);
- retirement or sheltered housing, with a warden or 'scheme manager' (see pages 94–95);
- an almshouse ;
- an Abbeyfield Society house;
- extra-care retirement housing; and
- housing for disabled people.

Almshouses

There are more than 30,000 almshouse dwellings in total throughout the UK. Most almshouses date back many centuries, having been provided by landowners and other benefactors for people in need of housing. Most of the accommodation has been fully modernised, and there are also newly built flats and bungalows, some of which are warden-assisted. A few almshouses can provide extra care for frail residents.

Normally almshouses only accept local applicants but exceptions can be made if the applicant has a connection with the area.

Residents do not have the same legal rights as tenants, for example in relation to rights to continue living in your home. If you or an older relative are thinking of moving into an almshouse, seek legal advice first.

For more information on local charities which administer almshouses, contact the Almshouse Association at the address on page 189.

Abbeyfield houses

Local Abbeyfield Societies manage about 800 houses throughout the UK. Abbeyfield houses cater for people looking for support in sheltered housing as well as opportunities for regular companionship. Most of the accommodation is in houses of six to ten unfurnished bedsitting rooms, with a shared lounge, dining room and garden. The weekly charge usually includes two main meals a day, prepared by a resident housekeeper, and facilities for residents to prepare their own breakfast and snacks.

Some Abbeyfield houses offer licences, but increasingly societies are offering tenancies rather than licenses. Seek advice about your rights before moving into an Abbeyfield house.

Details of your nearest Abbeyfield house can be obtained from the Abbeyfield Society at the address on page 188.

Extra-care retirement housing

Some councils and housing associations provide sheltered housing which offers extra care facilities. Such housing is for people who need personal care services, such as help with bathing or dressing. Accommodation is usually provided in self-contained flats, but unlike in sheltered housing there may be a shared dining room where meals are available. There may also be care staff to provide personal care.

Such housing is often run jointly with a local social services department and people will normally be housed there as a result of an assessment by a social services department (see page 169).

For more information on extra care schemes to rent or buy, contact the Elderly Accommodation Counsel at the address on page 189.

Housing for disabled people

Many local authorities and housing associations now have some properties that are specially built for people who use a wheelchair or have problems getting around. This may be referred to as 'mobility housing' or 'wheelchair housing'. Councils and housing associations are also encouraged to build 'lifetime' homes, which are designed to be adaptable to people's changing needs, including, for example, level access and downstairs toilet facilities.

Moving abroad

Many Britons dream of moving abroad to a warmer climate when they retire, and in recent years the number of people actually turning their dream into reality has risen significantly. If you are contemplating such a move, thorough research and planning is vital. You should consider all the pitfalls of moving house, as mentioned above – and more, as you could feel more isolated in another country.

There is a lot to be said for keeping your options open. You may well enjoy living abroad in the early years of retirement but may find that you wish to return to the UK as you get older and less active.

Keeping a UK base

Keeping your property in the UK will make it much easier to move back. If you sell your home, you may find yourself unable to afford a similar property on your return if property prices rise disproportionately in the UK.

If you decide to retain a UK base, you may consider letting your home while you are away. It is never a good idea for properties to stay empty for a long time, and the law makes it possible for owner-occupiers to let their property in the confidence of getting it back when they want it.

Renting rather than buying

Another way of keeping your options open is to rent rather than buy a home abroad. Renting gives you the chance to make sure that you like living abroad – and the location you have chosen – before you actually commit yourself to buying anything.

If you do decide to rent at least at first, you could try local estate agents (although there are not as many as in the UK), advertisements in local newspapers or, in a tourist area, the local tourist office, as you would for a long-stay holiday (see page 84).

Finding the right place

You have the right to live in any other European Economic Area (EEA) country – the EEA is made up of all EU countries plus Iceland, Liechtenstein and Norway. For non-EEA countries, the Foreign and Commonwealth Office recommends that you contact the British Consul abroad and the foreign consulate in the UK.

Be prepared to make more than one trip to the country you are thinking of moving to, and see as many properties as possible while you are there. Once you have chosen a place, it is always wise to try living there for at least a few months before committing yourself – both to experience the climate at different times of year and to get a general feel of what it is like to live there. The fact that you have enjoyed a holiday in a place does not mean you will enjoy living there permanently, especially if you went there some time ago – places change very rapidly. It is always worth talking to other people who have been retired there for some time.

Ask for advice from the foreign embassy in London. The local British Consul can supply lists of expatriate organisations. The Internet is also a good source of information.

Factors to bear in mind include:

- **Can you afford it?** You must be clear about your financial situation in retirement. House prices abroad may seem temptingly cheap, but you will have to live too. The rate of inflation in the country of your choice and fluctuations in exchange rates are factors beyond your control. Additional expenses to be considered are the costs of medical insurance and perhaps visits to the UK.
- **What about your pension** (see page 8) **and health costs abroad** (see page 87)?
- **Is it worth taking your furniture with you?** A specialist removal firm will be able to advise you about what items are not worth taking.
- **Can you take your pets?** Always ask your vet's advice first and make enquiries in the country you plan to visit. The Pet Travel Scheme (PETS) allows pet dogs and cats to re-enter the UK from certain countries without quarantine as long as they meet certain conditions.

Further information is available from DEFRA's PETS Helpline at the address on page 189.

- **Will you want to work?** You may have stated in your application for permanent residence that you do not intend to work. If you are offered part-time work, you should seek professional advice before accepting.

Buying property abroad

As far as finding a property is concerned, there are specialist magazines that cover homes for sale or to rent and holiday lettings and property developers are often represented at retirement exhibitions. In addition, many of the larger UK agents are now opening overseas departments.

The most essential rule for anyone buying property abroad is to take independent professional advice. If you do not speak the language, have someone who does with you at all the discussions.

Check that the local agent is a member of a recognised trade association working within the rules set by FOPDAC (the Federation of Overseas Property Developers, Agents and Consultants). Be wary of developers who say their lawyers have checked everything: you need a lawyer who is acting for you, and who puts your interests first. There are UK firms of solicitors who specialise in the purchase of foreign property.

The local British Consul can provide a list of English-speaking lawyers (or, if you have access to the Internet, a list is available on the Foreign and Commonwealth Office website at www.fco.gov.uk/travel).

Home security

If you want to remain where you are, there are various things that can be done to make the home feel safer and more secure.

Security precautions

The level of crime against older people is generally lower than for other age groups and the chances of you becoming a victim are also lower. Nonetheless, there are certain basic steps you can take to make your home more secure and to make yourself feel safer:

■ Make sure that the outside of the house is well lit.

■ Fit good locks on the front and back doors and all accessible windows. Do not ever leave them unlocked when you leave the house.

■ Have a door chain and a door viewer fitted to the front door, for use when answering the door. Always check the identity of a caller and the purpose of the visit before admitting them to your home. Don't leave the chain in position all the time, as this makes it more difficult to get help in an emergency.

■ Don't leave keys to doors or window locks anywhere a burglar might see them.

■ Don't keep large sums of money in the house.

It is generally not worth the expense of fitting a burglar alarm unless the local Crime Prevention Officer (CPO) advises this. The CPO will visit people at home and advise them how to make their home more secure.

Some local authorities and welfare organisations produce leaflets on security and crime prevention, and a few have special grant schemes to finance security measures. The local Age Concern, housing department or social services department should know if anything exists in the area. Home repair assistance might also be available from the local authority, as explained on page 113.

For more information about security measures, see Age Concern Factsheet 33 *Crime prevention for older people.*

Telephones

A telephone helps keep in touch with friends and get help in an emergency and is particularly valuable for people who are not able to get out very much. There is no national scheme providing financial help with telephones for older people. However, help with the costs of a telephone may be available in certain circumstances, including:

■ If you are chronically sick or disabled, the social services department may meet the cost of installation and sometimes the rental. Help with aids and adaptations to the telephone may also be available.

■ If you receive Income Support, you may be able to get a loan from the Social Fund (see pages 22–23) to meet installation costs.

■ If you make very few phone calls, you may benefit from a rebate on your phone rental under the BT 'Light User Scheme'.

You could also consider switching to an alternative telephone company that offers cheaper rates.

For more information, see Age Concern Factsheet 28 *Help with telephones.*

Alarms

Older people may worry about having an accident – falling over, for example – and being unable to call for help; and younger members of their family may worry about them. But people do not have to go into sheltered housing to have the security of a community or emergency alarm system.

Alarm systems allow you to be linked up 24 hours a day to a central control centre. The link is usually either by telephone, pull cord or a pendant which you wear round your neck – or a combination of these.

If you want to arrange for an older relative to have an alarm installed, contact the local housing department and social services department to see if either runs a community alarm scheme, and how much it costs. If they do not have a scheme, you may be able to consider buying an alarm. Those that are not connected to a control centre and do not allow two-way speech are not recommended.

 The Research Institute for Consumer Affairs (see page 186) has a publication on its website (www.ricability.org.uk) entitled *Calling for Help: A guide to community alarms.*

Repairs and improvements

When you retire you have a good opportunity to make a thorough assessment of the condition of your home. If repairs or maintenance are needed or are likely to be required in the next few years, or there are home improvements that you would like to make, it might be wise to get the work done now, when you may be able to do some of it yourself. You may decide to use some of the lump sum from an occupational or personal pension for this purpose.

Deciding what needs to be done

Home improvement agencies – often called 'Care and Repair' or 'Staying Put' – give specialist advice to older homeowners. They will normally offer practical help with such tasks as arranging a survey, getting estimates from reliable builders, applying for grants or building society loans, and keeping an eye on the work as it progresses. Agency services are non-profit-making, but they may charge a fee towards staff and other costs. This can normally be included in the grant or loan, if you are receiving one. Unfortunately, however, there is not a home improvement agency in every area.

 To find out if there is a home improvement agency in your area, contact your local Age Concern, your local council's housing department or *foundations* (the national co-ordinating body for home improvement agencies) at the address on page 190.

If there is no home improvement agency in your area, you may want to consider having a professional survey done by an architect or surveyor, especially if you live in an older property. Ask your local friends if they can recommend anyone. Before any surveyor inspects your property you should ask what the fee will be – you will have to pay this even if no repair work is carried out.

Contact your local CAB or the Royal Institution of Chartered Surveyors (at the address on page 191) for details of the Chartered Surveyors Voluntary Service, which aims to help people who would otherwise be unable to get professional advice. You will need to be referred to them by a CAB or other local advice agency.

The Royal Institute of British Architects (address on page 191) can help you find an architect.

If you are going to check things over yourself, you should look at the following areas:

Roof Inspect both outside (using binoculars) and inside (via the loft). Look out for broken or missing tiles, and inspect the supporting timbers for damp or white patches or any sign of woodworm or rot (the timber affected will be soft and spongy).

Chimney and external walls Look for signs of crumbling brickwork and cracking or damaged mortar. Rendered walls need to be repainted regularly (unless they have never been painted) and any loose rendering needs to be replaced. Make sure that air bricks are undamaged and clear of fallen leaves and soil.

Doors and windows All external paintwork needs regular repainting and the draught strip material may need replacing. Check window frames for damaged putty and rotten wood.

Guttering Cast-iron pipes should be repainted regularly – or replaced with plastic ones. Make sure that gutters are securely fixed and not blocked with leaves or dirt.

Plumbing Check all joints in pipes and fixtures to make sure that there are no leaks – white or green marks are a warning sign.

Wiring If your wiring is over 15 years old, have it checked by a professional electrician. If you get your home rewired, you might want to place new sockets at waist height. You might also want to consider some outside lighting, as this is a great deterrent to intruders.

Floors Check for signs of woodworm or dry rot.

Specialist firms will give you a free survey of floor and roof timbers. They will then guarantee any work carried out.

You can reduce your maintenance costs significantly by using good quality paint and building materials and by fitting items such as aluminium windows frames and doors that need almost no maintenance.

Finding a builder

If there is no home improvement agency service in your area, exercise great care when trying to find a good builder. Friends' recommendations may be fine for small jobs, but for larger ones you should always employ a builder backed by a proper guarantee scheme. With the Federation of Master Builders (FMB), you pay a premium equivalent to 1 per cent of the cost of the work, but it will probably be money well spent as their members must meet certain criteria and adhere to the Code of Practice.

 Information on the scheme, and a list of builders registered under it, can be obtained from the FMB at the address on page 189.

To ensure that you get a good job done the FMB recommends that you:

- Ask for references and names of previous clients.
- Get estimates from two or three different builders.
- Ask for the work to be covered by an insurance-backed warranty.
- Get a written specification and quotation.
- Use a contract (the FMB has simple forms of contract for small building work).
- Agree any staged and final payments before work starts.
- Avoid adding to or changing the job halfway through.
- Avoid dealing in cash.
- If any problems arise, talk to your builder straightaway.

Financial help with repairs and improvements

You may be able to get a home improvement grant from your local authority to help with the cost of repairs. However, the Government is in the process of making changes to the current grants system. Under new reforms the council no longer has to give home improvement grants or home repair assistance, but has to provide assistance to vulnerable and older homeowners to help them with repairs and improvements to their homes. There is a 12-month transitional period (from July 2002 to July 2003) during which authorities can continue to provide grants under the existing legislation. In the meantime, you will still have the right to apply for the existing grants. There are three types of grant:

Renovation grants help towards the cost of major repairs and improvements to your home, such as for home insulation or to provide adequate heating. All grants are discretionary: they will depend on your income and savings and the council's priorities.

Home repair assistance can help towards the cost of minor but essential repairs, improvements and adaptations, including improving energy efficiency and home security. The maximum grant is £5,000 for any one application. Help is available to anyone who is 'elderly, disabled or infirm' or in receipt of a means-tested benefit. Councils have considerable discretion in deciding who should get assistance.

Disabled facilities grants provide facilities and adaptations to help a disabled person to live as independently and in as much comfort as possible. They cover a wider range of work than renovation grants. If you qualify on income grounds, they will usually be mandatory (which means that the council must give them) if the home needs adaptations to enable someone to get in and out of it or to use essential facilities such as the bathroom, toilet, or kitchen.

Grants come from your local council (the one you pay your Council Tax to). Contact the renovation grants section in the housing or environmental health department. Never start any work before getting the council's approval or you will usually be unable to get a grant.

For more information on financial help with repairs, see Age Concern Factsheet 13 *Older homeowners: financial help with repairs and adaptations.* If there is a home improvement agency in your area, it should be able to give you advice on sources of financial help.

If you receive Income Support, you may be able to get a grant or loan from the Social Fund (see pages 22–23).

Social services departments provide funding for some types of minor adaptation works. They may also be able to help with the cost of work not covered by disabled facilities grants. The amount and type of help varies between councils.

For more information about the rights of disabled people to social services, see Age Concern Factsheet 32 *Disability and ageing: your rights to social services.*

If you cannot get a grant, or if you need additional money to top up the grant, you might be able to get an interest-only loan against the value of your home. These loans are normally from a building society or bank and are often intended specifically for older people. The market changes frequently, so shop around carefully. There is no tax relief on mortgage interest for loans for home improvements or repairs.

If you want to raise capital from your home specifically to pay for repairs, improvements or adaptations, the Home Improvement Trust may be able to help. It is a not-for-profit company which has special arrangements with commercial lenders who provide low cost loans to older people raised against the value of their home.

A local home improvement agency can refer you or you can contact the Trust direct at the address on page 190. (See pages 118–121 for information about schemes for raising money from the value of your home.)

Insulation and draughtproofing

It is well worth considering what you can do to reduce heat loss from your home, both for your own comfort and to save on heating bills.

Draughtproofing As much as a quarter of all heat lost from homes is through draughts from floors, doors and windows. Draughtproofing doors and windows (but not in kitchens and bathrooms), and sealing gaps between the skirting and the floor and around pipes and cables, will all help to reduce this heat loss.

Loft insulation A further quarter of all heat loss is through the roof. You should have insulation material of at least 100 mm (4 in) and preferably 150 mm (6 in) thick between the ceiling joists. This usually comes in a form of a glass-fibre quilt. If you do fit this yourself you should always wear a dust mask and gloves. Make sure you:

■ insulate hot and cold water pipes and tanks, but not underneath the cold water tank, since warmth from below will help stop it freezing;
■ insulate and draughtproof the loft hatch; and
■ leave sufficient air-gaps between the eaves to avoid condensation, which can rot timbers.

Wall insulation In an average semi-detached house walls lose more heat than any other part of the home. If your house has unfilled cavity walls, having them insulated will cut down your heating bills enormously. You will need a contractor to do this. If cavity wall insulation is not possible, you could consider insulating the walls on the inside or outside, but this is much more expensive. Lining the walls behind radiators with foil or aluminium sheets can help reduce heat loss, particularly on external walls.

Windows In addition to draughtproofing, you can reduce heat loss through windows by insulating using heavy, lined curtains (behind not in front of radiators) and fitting shelves above radiators under windows – about 75 mm (3 in) above is a good way to prevent heat loss. Double glazing is a good idea if you are replacing windows anyway. Otherwise you can fit secondary glazing – a single pane of glass – to your windows. Plastic glazing material clipped on to your windows – or even thin plastic film taped on – is cheaper, but it needs to be replaced regularly and looks unattractive.

Doors Apart from draughtproofing, you can reduce heat loss by fixing a cover to the inside of your letter box, hanging a curtain over the door and attaching draught strips (brushes) to the bottom of the door – or you can use a traditional sausage dog.

Hot water cylinder jacket Fitting a hot water cylinder jacket can pay for itself almost in a matter of weeks provided it is thick enough (at least 75 mm).

Advice on getting insulation or draughtproofing work carried out is available from EAGA Partnership Ltd at the address on page 189.

Financial help with insulation and draughtproofing

Householders aged 60 and over who are on an income-related benefit can apply for a Warm Front Grant (previously the Home Energy Efficiency Scheme). As well as offering a range of insulation measures it will also, where appropriate, provide high energy efficiency central heating systems for the main living areas. The maximum grant is £2,500. The grants are targeted at eligible owner occupiers and tenants in private rented accommodation. In some areas households receiving a grant will also have an assessment conducted on the security of their home.

 For more information about the grants and how to apply, ring Freephone 0800 316 6011. The rules are different in Wales and Scotland (Freephone 0800 072 0150).

You may be able to get home repair assistance from your local authority to help with the cost of insulation and draughtproofing (see page 113).

Ventilation

Open fires, gas fires, flued boilers and flueless appliances (such as paraffin or bottled gas heaters and gas cookers) all need a good supply of fresh air to burn safely and efficiently. You can ensure that there is a good supply of air into the room by fitting an air brick or trickle ventilator.

Lack of ventilation can also lead to condensation. The poorer the ventilation and the colder the home, the greater the risk. As much moisture as possible should be removed by:

- opening windows while cooking or drying clothes;
- fitting trickle ventilators or an extractor fan; and
- not draughtproofing kitchen or bathroom windows (but you can draughtproof the internal doors to keep moisture from spreading through the house).

Heating

Having ensured that your home is well insulated, it is sensible to consider whether your heating system is energy-efficient and economical to run. If you do not have central heating, you should consider installing it. If your central heating boiler is more than ten years old, it may be worth replacing it: one of the new energy-efficient ones could reduce your fuel bills by as much as 10–15 per cent.

An older central heating system may have rather basic controls. More sophisticated controls – set at different temperatures at different times of day – could save you money. Fitting thermostats to radiators or time clocks to individual heaters could also help.

Sources of help and advice

Both gas and electricity companies offer advice on the best way to use appliances and how to make your heating system more efficient. Telephone the customer services number on your fuel bill to arrange for an adviser to visit.

All gas and electricity suppliers are required to give priority services on request and without charge to people of pensionable age, people with disabilities and the chronically sick. These include special controls or adapters and a free annual gas safety check. In addition, they should not cut off supplies for non payment of bills during the winter months. To obtain these services, you must apply to the supplier to be included on their register of people who qualify.

Remember that you can now have your gas and electricity supplied by a company of your choice. Changing supplier may lead to lower bills and better quality of service.

For more information, see Age Concern Factsheet 1 *Help with heating*. For information leaflets on how to choose a supplier and a factsheet giving price comparisons, contact Ofgem at the address on page 191. Energywatch, the Consumer Council, is also a useful source of information – the helpline number is 0845 906 0708.

Raising income or capital from your home

Equity release schemes enable older homeowners to raise extra income or a cash lump sum from their homes. The younger you are when you begin one of these plans the longer it has to run and the greater the care you have to take to make sure that it is suitable for your needs now and in the future.

Home reversion schemes

The most common form of equity release scheme is a home reversion scheme. With these schemes you sell your home, or a part of your home, to a private company called a reversion company. In return you receive a cash lump sum or a monthly annuity income and you continue to live in the house as a tenant rather than the full owner. When the property is sold, usually after your death, the reversion company receives its percentage of the proceeds of the sale.

On your death the company receives the full value of the part of the property you have sold, including any appreciation in value on that part. You normally remain responsible for any repairs and maintenance and pay a nominal rent.

When you sell all or part of your home to a reversion company, you don't receive full market value – you normally only get between a third and a half – this is because the reversion company gives you the right to live in your home for the rest of your life. The percentage of the market value that you receive depends on your age and sex. Older people get more than younger people, and men get more than women, because they have lower life expectancies.

Roll-up loans

Over the last few years a number of new style roll-up loans have been introduced. With a roll-up loan, you take out a loan against the value of your home. Unlike with normal mortgages, you do not have to make any repayments of interest or capital until you sell your home. Instead, the interest is 'rolled up' and added to the total loan.

Most schemes now provide fixed interest rates with a guarantee that the loan will never go beyond a certain level. Nevertheless, it is crucial to be aware of how quickly the debt can accumulate. For example, a loan will roughly double every 10 years if the interest rate is 7.5 per cent. Only consider these schemes if the interest rate is fixed for life and even then be extremely cautious about how much you borrow.

Home income plans

With a home income plan (HIP) you also continue to occupy your home and you mortgage your property for part of its capital value and use the proceeds to buy a lifetime annuity. The interest payments on the loan are deducted from this monthly income. The capital is repaid from the proceeds of the sale of your home, usually after you die.

There is no mortgage interest tax relief on HIPs taken out after March 1999 and so the amount of money you can raise from a HIP is very limited. This makes HIPs much less financially attractive to most people, although they may be worth considering for single people in their late 70s and over, and for couples in their 80s.

Other schemes

If you do not think that one of these schemes would suit you, you may be able to take out a loan or mortgage using the value of your home as security.

Ordinary loans The disadvantage of ordinary loans is that repayments are likely to be fairly high, and you may find some companies unwilling to lend to you because of your age.

Interest-only loans These are available from some banks and building societies. You pay only interest and the loan is repaid on your death or when you sell the property – although the mortgage can generally be transferred to another suitable property. However, the interest payments could still be fairly high.

Points to consider

It is always a good idea to get independent legal and financial advice before taking out an equity release scheme. Think carefully about what your needs really are. Some of the factors you should think about include:

- **How old do I have to be?** Age limits do vary, but there are only a few schemes open to people under the age of 65. For couples, the limit is more likely to be 70.
- **What conditions will I have to meet?** These will vary between companies and different schemes, but may include a maximum loan and a minimum property value (this varies but is often £40,000 or £50,000).
- **Will my State benefits be affected?** If you are receiving an income-related benefit such as Income Support (Minimum Income Guarantee) or Council Tax Benefit, the scheme income could mean that you lose all or some of your benefits.
- **How much will I have to pay in fees, costs and commission?**
- **What would the position be if I want to move house?**
- **Do I need capital protection?** You should think about what would happen if you died soon after taking out a scheme.

Make sure that you have the scheme details in writing, including the answers to your questions.

Legal protection

There is no specific regulatory body for companies selling these schemes. Companies providing an annuity income rather than a lump sum are regulated by the Financial Services Authority (see page 35). Roll-up loans and reversion schemes based on a lump sum are not – it is therefore very important to get independent legal and financial advice. Mortgages and loans are due to be directly regulated by the FSA but this is not expected to be fully implemented before 2004.

Some companies are members of the SHIP (Safe Home Income Plans) campaign and agree to operate by a voluntary code of practice. They use a ship logo on their printed literature.

If you are considering a loan, ask whether the company subscribes to the Code of Mortgage Lending Practice which is run by the Council of Mortgage Lenders.

For detailed advice about raising income or capital from your home, see the Age Concern Books annual publication *Using Your Home As Capital* (details on page 199).

For details of companies offering schemes, see Age Concern Factsheet 12 *Raising income or capital from your home.*

Staying healthy

If you retire at around 60 you may have a third of your life ahead of you. How much you get out of it will depend partly on your state of health, so retirement seems a good time to give some thought to your body and to making sure it is in as good shape as possible for the years to come.

This chapter looks at what you can do to achieve a healthy lifestyle. It also outlines some common health problems and includes a summary of the help that is available with health costs.

- **Looking after your body**
- **Health problems**
- **Help with health costs**

Looking after your body

Many people who lead busy working lives neglect their bodies over the years. They may not have time for regular exercise, they may often find themselves falling back on convenience foods, they may never have found the ideal moment to give up smoking. People often tend to feel that by the time they reach retirement the damage has already been done and it is not worth making the effort to change. But it is never too late: positive benefits can be reaped from changes in your lifestyle whatever your age.

Taking exercise

Research has shown that people who remain fit and active are healthier and less likely to die of heart disease and a range of other illnesses than those who take less exercise. Generally, it is the years of inactivity, rather than ageing as such, that cause the deterioration in physical fitness.

The good news is that fitness can be regained: almost everyone over the age of 50, whatever their health problems, can benefit from exercise provided it is gentle and safe. If you start exercising regularly in retirement, you may end up fitter than you have been for years.

There are many advantages to taking regular exercise as you get older, including:

- It makes you feel more energetic and alert.
- It helps keep you supple and prevents stiffness in your spine and joints.
- It maintains muscle and bone strength.
- It helps keep your weight under control.
- It helps prevent osteoporosis (which mainly affects women but does also affect men – see pages 145–146) and many common illnesses.
- It can make you feel better and look better. How you hold yourself, your complexion and your shape could all improve.

No matter how late in life you begin to increase the amount of exercise you do, you will notice benefits. If you have always taken regular exercise, obviously all you need to do is carry on – even if you do find it gradually more difficult than you used to. Retirement could also provide an ideal opportunity for you to try some other sporting activity you have never done before.

What exercise is suitable?

People who don't like the idea of exercise will often cite the proverbial case of the 55-year-old first-time jogger who drops down dead in his tracks. If you have a health problem or haven't exercised for years, it is obviously wise to check with your GP first, and to increase the length and intensity of your activity gradually. Stop immediately if you feel any unpleasant effects such as pain or dizziness. A good rule of thumb is that you should be able to talk to someone while you are exercising.

Activities to avoid for people who are not fit and active are those which involve too much exertion or strain. Squash, jogging and aerobics might be too strenuous for the unfit – as well as jarring to the knees and hips. Both walking and swimming are ideal all-round forms of exercise. Table tennis, short-mat bowling and racquetball are all sociable indoor activities that do not require too much exertion and are ideal for the less fit. Remember, however, that far more older people suffer from the effects of inactivity than hurt themselves by taking exercise.

Any vigorous exercise session should start with a gradual warm-up. This means that you get the circulation going and get oxygenised blood into the muscles and joints before performing more vigorous actions. It's also good to start and finish with some stretching exercises. This helps keep you supple and reduces the risk of injury. Only stretch as much as is comfortable and never bounce while doing a stretch. Wait until two hours after eating before you start, and have a glass of water every half hour.

Walking regularly (and briskly) provides good exercise – although it does not do much to increase suppleness. Try to walk 1–2 miles a day, at a speed that accelerates the heartbeat and warms the body. If you get bored with the same old route every day, you could try a guided walk occasionally. There are usually leaflets in libraries giving dates and meeting places and a rough idea of the distance. For longer walks you could see if there is a Ramblers' Association group locally (the national address is on page 186).

Swimming is an excellent all-round form of exercise: it uses many different muscles as well as stimulating the heart and circulation. It is particularly good for people with arthritis as the water supports the body and takes the weight off painful joints. It is not, however, as helpful in the prevention of osteoporosis as weight-bearing exercise such as walking.

You don't have to be able to swim already: many pools offer special classes for older non-swimmers. If you already swim well, you might like to take a life-saving certificate, or help at a swimming session for disabled people.

Cycling is the most energy-efficient way of getting about, and it is also good exercise. It doesn't matter if you haven't done it for years: as with swimming, once you have learned you never forget.

Cycling in big towns in heavy traffic can be both dangerous and unpleasant but, if you wear a helmet and choose the right roads and the right time of day, cycling is a good way to get about. Town planners are increasingly trying to provide cycle lanes and cycle routes, and local cycling groups publish route maps which avoid main roads.

Once you have built up confidence with local trips, you might like to arm yourself with Ordinance Survey maps and explore the surrounding countryside. If you prefer the idea of cycling in a group, the Cyclists' Touring Club will give you details of local activities as well as technical advice.

 For more information, contact the Cyclists' Touring Club at the address on page 181.

Exercise classes

Exercise classes provide an opportunity to keep fit with expert supervision and in congenial company. Most leisure and sports centres run keep-fit classes for the over-50s, as do adult education services and some local Age Concerns. Some run sessions for women only.

Dancing in all its forms is not only fun but also provides good exercise. Another popular activity among older people is Tai-chi. Originally a Chinese martial art, it consists of a series of slow choreographed movements and helps to improve muscle strength, balance and breathing. Yoga and Pilates involve stretching, relaxation and breath control and are good ways of improving posture, breathing and suppleness.

Exercising at home

If you don't like the idea of joining a class, you can exercise at home, to the accompaniment of a tape, video or keep-fit programme on television.

If you are contemplating buying an exercise machine, an exercise bike is useful and versatile, although many people get bored with them and find they hardly ever use them. It is worth checking that the machine is stable and does not rock as you use it.

You can also try to include more exercise in your daily life by walking or cycling rather than taking the bus or car or by walking up stairs in shops and offices rather than using escalators or lifts.

For more information, see Age Concern Factsheet 45 *Fitness for later life*. The Age Concern publication *Alive and Kicking* (see page 200) has suggestions on exercise for people with mobility problems.

Eating well

There is no shortage of leaflets and posters telling us about the kinds of foods we should be eating. We are probably all aware that we should be reducing fat, sugar and salt in our diet and eating more fibre-rich foods and more fruit and vegetables (five portions a day). This does not mean that we have all followed this advice and made the necessary changes – although many people have made changes in their eating habits in recent years.

Less fat

A small amount of fat in the diet is essential, but most of us should eat less of it. Eating less has two main advantages:

- As fat is extremely high in calories, eating less will help you lose weight if you need to.
- Cutting down on saturated fats – mainly animal fats – reduces the level of cholesterol in the blood and so lessens the risk of coronary heart disease and other conditions.

We are therefore advised to grill rather than fry, trim all visible fat from meat, use all fats sparingly, and switch to semi-skimmed or skimmed milk and low-fat products. When frying food, it is recommended that you use an oil that is high in unsaturates, such as olive oil or sunflower oil. Remember that there is hidden fat in foods such as crisps, cakes and chocolate.

At the same time we are told to eat more oily fish, which is rich in polyunsaturates and other nutritional elements that are thought to be beneficial. These are believed to help reduce the tendency of the blood to clot, so lessening the risk of thrombosis and heart attacks.

Less sugar

For people who love chocolate, cakes and biscuits, cutting down on sugar is not easy, but the advantages are all too obvious:

■ As sugar is high in calories, eating less will help you lose weight if this is needed. The calories in sugar are 'empty' ones: sugar contains calories but has no food value.

■ Sugar is a prime cause of tooth decay and gum disease.

Much of the sugar we eat is hidden in that it is added to foods such as baked beans and breakfast cereals. It is worth checking on food labels to see whether sugar has been added and how much (ingredients are always listed in order of quantity).

Less salt

Although the links between large amounts of salt in the diet and high blood pressure have not been proved conclusively, it is recommended that people should cut down on their consumption of salt as much as they possibly can.

Cut down on salt by reducing gradually the amount used in cooking or sprinkled on food. Herbs and spices reduce the need for salt. Cutting down on salty snacks and preserved foods such as bacon, ham and sausages will also help. Other salty foods used in cooking include stock cubes and soy sauce.

More fibre

Wholemeal bread, wholegrain breakfast cereals, beans, lentils, fruit and vegetables are rich in fibre (roughage). There are two types of fibre, both vitally important:

■ The type which predominates in cereals is needed to keep the bowel system working and avoid constipation.
■ The type which predominates in beans, oats, fruit and vegetables may help correct blood cholesterol levels.

It is said that most people in Britain need to increase their intake of fibre by eating more fruit and vegetables and more starchy foods such as bread, cereals, pasta, potatoes and rice. These foods are a good source of energy and an essential part of a balanced diet.

Vitamins and minerals

Vitamin and mineral supplements will not usually be necessary if you:

■ eat a variety of foods, including plenty of fruit and vegetables;
■ ensure that the food you eat is fresh – storing food properly will help keep it fresh; and
■ cook vegetables for a short time in as little water as possible or steam them.

Sometimes, however, supplements are necessary because of an illness such as anaemia; they are then best prescribed by a doctor.

Check with your doctor first before making drastic changes to your diet, especially if you have a condition such as diabetes.

Fluids

The body needs two litres of fluid a day in order to function properly. In particular, constipation can be aggravated by not drinking enough.

Water is best and most beneficial: it is recommended that everyone drinks two litres (eight glasses) a day – that does not include tea or coffee as these are diuretics.

Alcohol

Alcohol is part of many people's eating and drinking pattern and is fine in moderation. The average recommended guidelines for weekly alcohol consumption are 14–21 units for women and 21–28 units for men, spread through the week. (Half a pint of beer, lager or cider, one small glass of wine, sherry or port, or one measure of spirits each comprise one unit.) However, these limits may be much too high as you get older, as tolerance of alcohol seems to decrease with age.

While drinking too much can cause blood pressure to rise and eventually cause liver damage, there is some evidence that people who drink small amounts of alcohol regularly may protect against some illnesses, such as coronary heart disease.

 For confidential information, help and advice about drinking, telephone Drinkline at the number on page 193.

Avoiding food poisoning

There have been many alarms about food safety in recent years.

Salmonella The most common cause of food poisoning is probably salmonella bacteria, particularly associated with poultry and eggs. The bacteria are killed when food is thoroughly cooked. When cooking or reheating it is therefore vital that foods are heated until they are piping hot.

This should not present a problem with poultry, which should be thoroughly defrosted before cooking and should always be served cooked right through. However, eggs are often served lightly cooked, as in scrambled eggs, or raw, as in chocolate mousse. You should avoid lightly cooked or raw eggs if you come under one of the Department of Health's 'at risk' categories. These 'at risk' categories include frail older people, those who are ill or convalescent and those with reduced resistance to infection, either because they are taking medicines which suppress the body's natural immunity or because of a condition such as HIV or diabetes.

Another useful precaution is to ensure that raw eggs and poultry do not contaminate other food. It is a good idea to keep raw meat and poultry at the bottom of the fridge to make sure that it does not drip on to other foods, and to make sure that chopping boards and utensils are cleaned thoroughly.

Listeria There is only a very small risk of a healthy person contracting listeriosis. However, listeria bacteria can continue to multiply at fridge temperature, so it is wise for anyone in an 'at risk' category to avoid all foods likely to contain high levels of the bacteria. These include:

- raw unpasteurised milk;
- soft mould-ripened cheese, such as Brie, Camembert and Danish blue;
- pre-cooked chilled meals and roasted poultry;
- meat, fish or vegetable pâté; and
- soft-whip ice cream from machines.

E Coli While forms of E Coli are found naturally in the human gut, the lethal form that leads to food poisoning outbreaks occurs mainly in beef. As with salmonella, the bacteria are killed by thorough cooking, which is especially important with all forms of minced beef, hamburgers, etc. As mentioned above, it is a good idea to keep raw meat at the bottom of the fridge and to be scrupulous about cleaning knives and chopping boards.

See Age Concern Books' *Eating Well on a Budget* for more tips about safe handling and storing of food and for a week's lunch and supper recipes for each season of the year. *Healthy Eating on a Budget* explains the principles of healthy eating and provides over 100 recipes (see details on page 201).

Pesticides

You may have concerns about pesticide residues in food. The newer pesticides now in use remain in the environment for shorter periods than earlier ones, and residue levels are thought to be low.

Careful washing or peeling removes some pesticides, but not systemic pesticides that are absorbed by the cells of the plant. If you want to avoid residues it is best to buy organic food, grown without any deliberate application of pesticides.

Losing weight

Being overweight when you're older increases the risk of diabetes, high blood pressure, heart disease and varicose veins and puts additional stress on your joints, particularly your knees and hips.

Your metabolic rate (ie, the rate at which your body processes what you eat and drink) slows gradually as the years pass; keeping your figure requires a gradual reduction of calorie intake. Being overweight is the result of an imbalance between calorie intake and energy output. Doing some exercise should also help. The easiest way to take in fewer calories is to follow the basic principles of healthy eating: less fat, sugar and salt and more fibre-rich foods.

You might find joining a weight-watching club useful. Do make sure, however, that the organisation you join is reputable and encourages healthy eating and exercise rather than rapid weight loss through special diets or diet foods. What you should be aiming for is permanent weight loss, which can come about only through a change in your energy needs or eating habits.

Smoking

It has long been known that smoking causes lung cancer, coronary heart disease, chronic bronchitis and emphysema. It is now recognised that it is also a cause of strokes, arteriosclerosis (the build-up of fatty tissues and loss of elasticity in the arteries) and other cancers, including cancer of the mouth, and that it is a contributory factor in yet more diseases. It also affects your general fitness and makes you more inclined to get out of breath.

Giving up will benefit your health whatever your age, however long you have been smoking and whether you smoke cigarettes, cigars or a pipe. Ten to fifteen years after giving up, an ex-smoker's risk of developing lung cancer is only slightly greater than that of someone who has never smoked, and the relative risk of a heart attack is reduced to almost that of a non-smoker.

The best way is usually to give up completely rather than trying to cut down gradually. It may help to analyse when you smoke. If you smoke after meals, for example, try to break the habit by washing the dishes or going for a walk before you reach for a cigarette. Many people find giving up easier than expected and the worst withdrawal symptoms are generally over in a month. Within a few weeks your hair, skin and breath will stop smelling of tobacco smoke and your breathing will improve, as will your sense of taste and smell.

If you feel you need outside help, the NHS smoking cessation service is free and provides a range of support – contact your GP or NHS Direct (address on page 193).

Quitline is a national telephone helpline (see page 193) for smokers who need advice or help in stopping. It will give you details of your nearest stop-smoking group and can send you an information Quitpack.

Dental care

Gone are the days when everyone expected to lose all their own teeth and wear dentures instead. Improvements in dental techniques mean that it is now possible to fill or crown almost any tooth. Teeth are more likely to be lost through advanced gum disease, which is much more difficult to treat.

Gum disease is caused by ineffective cleaning of the teeth, leaving plaque in areas where teeth and gums meet. Bacteria in plaque 'feed' off the food we eat and produce waste products that cause inflammation of the gums and eventually loosening of the teeth. The first sign of gum disease is when gums bleed easily.

Receding of the gums due to gum disease cannot be reversed, but it can be halted. To prevent gum disease and tooth decay:

- Brush teeth thoroughly daily with a medium-texture, small-headed brush – dentists suggests this should take at least five minutes.
- Use dental floss or wooden dental sticks – you can ask your dentist or hygienist for advice.
- Use a toothpaste containing fluoride.
- Cut down your intake of sugar, which converts into acid in the mouth and attacks your teeth. To cut down the number of times you eat sugar, dentists usually recommend that you keep sugar containing foods to mealtimes.
- Go to your dentist for a check-up at least once a year.

It is a good idea to go to a dentist once a year even if you have none of your own teeth left. Gums naturally change shape when the teeth have been removed, at first rapidly and then more slowly, so dentures need to be adjusted and sometimes replaced. The discomfort many people report with their dentures may well be because they are wearing ill-fitting or broken dentures that should have been replaced years ago.

Brushing dentures properly is extremely important as plaque builds up on dentures as well as teeth, and can cause the tissues underneath to become infected. When you take your dentures out you should always keep them wet; if the plastic is allowed to dry out, the dentures may warp.

Obtaining dental care

In some areas it can be very difficult to find an NHS dentist near to your home. It is a good idea to make sure you are registered with a dentist for regular treatment (called 'continuing care'). This entitles you to all the care and treatment required in order to maintain oral health and emergency dental treatment if necessary.

Before each course of treatment, the patient and dentist should discuss any treatment that is proposed and what it will cost. The dentist will usually draw up a 'treatment plan'; if this does not happen, you can always ask for one.

Continuing care arrangements between patient and dentist last 15 months and can then be renewed. You can sign on with any dentist you like provided that they are taking NHS patients and are willing to accept you.

For advice on how to find an NHS dentist, contact NHS Direct at the number on page 193.

Paying for dental care

You will generally pay 80 per cent of the costs of all treatment, up to a ceiling of £366 for any one course of treatment (2002 figure: £354 in Wales). If you are on Income Support you are entitled to exemption from NHS dental charges. If you have a low income, you may be entitled to free treatment or some help with the costs, as explained on page 147.

There are no set fees for private treatment, nor is there any help towards private dental fee from NHS sources.

 For more information about dental care, see Age Concern Factsheet 5 *Dental care and older people.*

Looking after your feet

Many adults have foot problems, often as a result of wearing ill-fitting shoes. It makes sense to start looking after your feet from now on: if they are not in good shape it will be harder for you to remain active as you get older.

To help keep your feet in good condition:

- Wash them daily, making sure you dry them thoroughly.
- Remove any build-up of hard skin with a pumice stone.
- Rub in cream, exercising your toes as you do so.
- Exercise your ankles by rotating your feet, once at a time, first in a clockwise and then in an anti-clockwise direction.

Cutting your toenails Toenails dry out and become harder to cut as you get older. Immediately after bathing is a good time to cut them as the water makes them softer. An alternative is to file them with an emery board. Always consult a chiropodist if you have painful or ingrowing toenails.

Aching feet If your feet are aching and swollen at the end of the day, it may help to lie or sit down with your feet raised higher than your hips for about 15 minutes. Dipping tired feet alternately, for a minute at a time, in warm and then cold water will help the circulation. Try not to sit with your legs or ankles crossed for too much of the time, as this restricts the circulation.

Inflamed, swollen or painful feet You should consult a doctor if any part of your foot becomes inflamed, swollen or painful or if the skin becomes white, dusky red or purple, because the blood circulation to the foot may be affected.

Corns and calluses It is advisable to have these treated by a chiropodist, particularly if you have circulation problems or a condition such as diabetes which leaves you more prone to infections.

Chiropody

NHS chiropody services are free to anyone over the age of 65, but the extent of provision varies in different parts of the country. To find out about your local NHS chiropody service, ask at your GP's surgery or telephone NHS Direct at the number on page 193. The NHS employs only state-registered chiropodists, who use the letters SRCh after their names.

If you wish to consider private treatment, your local NHS chiropody service may have details. Alternatively, you may wish to refer to *Yellow Pages*.

Hair loss

While many men suffer what is known as pattern baldness – a receding hairline and thinning on the crown – women may experience overall thinning. Some people with thinning hair may find a change of hairstyle helps, but others may consider more radical solutions.

There are many different methods of hair replacement, surgical and non-surgical. Impartial advice can be obtained from a qualified trichologist.

For general advice on hair and scalp problems, write to the Institute of Trichologists at the address on page 193. It can send you a list of registered member trichologists in your area; it also publishes several leaflets, including one on general hair care and another on consulting a trichologist.

Wigs and fabric supports are supplied through hospitals and are free for in-patients. If you are an out-patient, there are charges unless you are receiving Income Support or have a low income (see page 147).

Health problems

Most people are likely to stay fit and active well into their 80s. Some may encounter new health concerns, such as high blood pressure or heart disease, and have to watch what they eat to a greater extent than before or take exercise more regularly. With a little care, most such conditions need not be a bar to a fulfilling lifestyle. This section looks at some of the more common health problems that can affect people as they get older, with the emphasis on preventative measures and positive ways of coping. If you want more information, there are many organisations that offer advice and information about specific illnesses and disabilities.

Factfile

■ In 2000, 57 per cent of people aged 65–74 and 64 per cent of people aged 75 and over had a long-standing illness. Of those aged between 65 and 74, 37 per cent and, of those aged over 75, 47 per cent, said that the illness limited their lifestyle.

Arthritis

There are three main types of arthritis: rheumatoid arthritis, which can come on in middle age; osteoarthritis, which is common in old age; and gout, which – contrary to popular belief – is not caused by excessive drinking.

Osteoarthritis affects nearly 70 per cent of women and nearly 60 per cent of men aged over 65. Certain changes in the cartilage of joints cause pain and stiffness and restrict activity. It runs in families to some extent and joints that are already damaged seem most likely to be affected. Abnormal wear and tear and being overweight make things worse.

You can help prevent further injury by:

■ keeping your weight down, thus reducing the pressure on joints;
■ keeping yourself mobile; and
■ exercising as much as possible without straining a painful joint.

Swimming is particularly good, as is cycling, provided that the arthritis is not too severe. Exercise that jolts the joints, such as jogging or aerobics, should be avoided.

There are various things you can do to try to ease aching, painful joints:

■ Rest a painful joint, especially after standing for long periods. Balance rest with activity – too much rest can cause muscle stiffness.

■ Keep the affected area warm with a covered hot water bottle or heated pad.

■ Take painkillers – but you should consult a doctor if you need to take them more than once or twice a week.

In severe cases the doctor may arrange physiotherapy, or replacement of the damaged joint with an artificial one. Hip replacements are now common and safe, and knee replacements increasingly so.

 For more information, contact Arthritis Care at the address on page 191.

 See also the Age Concern Books publication *Caring for someone with arthritis* (details on page 202). For more information about aids and adaptations in the home for people with disabilities, see pages 168–169.

Cancer

If diagnosed and treated early enough, many cancers can be completely cured. Sadly, many people do not report symptoms until the cancer is far advanced. Symptoms that should be reported to a doctor immediately include:

■ passing blood in vomit, sputum, faeces or urine, or from the vagina;
■ unexplained weight loss or loss of appetite;
■ hoarseness that persists for more than two weeks or a persistent cough;
■ persistent indigestion or difficulty in swallowing;
■ an unusual lump in the breast or armpit or a change in the shape or size of the breast or in the colour of the nipple;

- a sore on the lips, tongue or face that takes more than two weeks to heal or is getting bigger;
- lumps or tenderness in the testicles or difficulty passing urine (which can be signs of prostate cancer);
- a mole that is itching, inflamed, bleeding or crusting, or growing in size (which can be a sign of skin cancer); or
- an unexplained change in bowel habits.

As there are several hundred different types of cancer, this list is by no means comprehensive.

All women should be screened for cervical cancer by means of a smear test every three to five years until the clinic advises that further ones are unnecessary. Women between 50 and 70 are also entitled to a free mammography (breast X-ray) about every three years or so. Screening is generally organised by your GP. If you are over 70 and wish to continue having mammograms, you can ask for this to be done.

There is no organised screening programme for prostate cancer, but GPs are being sent information packs to try to ensure that men who are concerned about the risk of prostate cancer receive clear and balanced information. A pilot colorectal (bowel) cancer screening programme is taking place in some parts of the UK but is not yet available in all areas.

Copies of the NHS leaflets *Breast screening: an informed choice* and *Cervical screening: an informed choice* are available from the NHS Response Line on 08701 555 455. For more information about the NHS screening programmes, see the website at www.cancerscreening.nhs.uk

For information and advice about cancer, contact CancerLink at the address on page 192.

For information, advice and counselling about breast cancer or other breast-related problems, contact Breast Cancer Care at the address on page 192.

See also the Age Concern Books publication *Caring for someone with cancer* (details on page 202).

Diabetes

Diabetes often develops in older people when the pancreas fails to produce enough insulin, or the insulin it does produce cannot work properly. Insulin is needed to help the body use sugar to produce energy.

Some people suffer the symptoms of diabetes – including tiredness, blurred vision, weight changes, thirst and passing water more frequently than usual – but put them down to other things. If you think you might have diabetes, your doctor can do a simple on-the-spot blood or urine test. You are more 'at risk' if you are overweight and unfit. African-Caribbean or South Asian people are three to five times more likely to have diabetes than white members of the population.

There is no cure for diabetes but it can be successfully treated. The type of diabetes that commonly develops in older people does not usually require insulin but everyone with diabetes is encouraged to eat healthily. A healthy, balanced diet is low in fat, sugar and salt, with plenty of fruit and vegetables and meals based on starchy carbohydrate foods like bread, potatoes, pasta and chapattis. Your local healthcare team (doctor, dietician, and nurse) will give you advice.

If you have diabetes, you should pay particular attention to foot care, as minor cuts or abrasions can lead to a serious infection. It is advisable to visit the chiropodist regularly for a check-up. As a diabetic, you will be entitled to free sight tests. It is very important that you have an annual medical examination which includes a check on eyesight and an examination of the back of the eye.

For information and advice about diabetes, including a wide range of leaflets, contact Diabetes UK at the address on page 192.

See also the Age Concern Books publication *Caring for someone with diabetes* (details on page 202).

Eye problems

The only 'normal' ageing change in the eye is that the lens tends to lose its elasticity; as a result older people often need glasses for reading.

Other changes are not normal and should be discussed with your GP. Some older people develop one of three common eye diseases:

■ cataract (a clouding of the lens);
■ glaucoma (when the fluid inside the eyeball increases); or
■ macular degeneration (which affects the retina).

Diabetes can also impair your sight. Cataract and glaucoma are both treatable, and laser treatment can often halt the changes that occur in diabetes.

You should have a sight test every year, and sooner if you notice changes in your eyesight. Sight tests are free for people aged 60 and over.

For details about help with the cost of glasses for people with low incomes, see page 147.

The Royal National Institute of the Blind (address on page 193) offers advice and information for people with eye problems.

Hearing problems

Some loss of ability to hear high-pitched sounds, such as the telephone, is common as people get older. If you are unable to follow a conversation with several people talking, or experience other problems with your hearing, consult your GP.

If hearing difficulties are not due to wax in the ear or an ear infection, your GP may refer you to the hearing clinic of the local hospital where an accurate diagnosis can be made. After your consultation, you may be prescribed a hearing aid. NHS hearing aids are available on free loan; replacements and batteries are also free. Initially some people dislike the way that hearing aids amplify background sounds as well as what they actually want to hear, but it is usually worth persevering.

The Royal National Institute for Deaf People (address on page 193) produces a range of information leaflets on hearing loss, hearing aids, tinnitus (ringing in the ears) and other issues.

Heart disease

Heart disease usually develops before people are 65, although symptoms may not appear until later, so prevention should start much earlier. To reduce the likelihood of heart disease developing, or to prevent an already existing heart condition getting worse, there are various things you can do:

- Stop smoking.
- Keep your weight steady, or lose some if you are overweight.
- Reduce your overall intake of fat and switch to more unsaturated fats.
- Take exercise – swimming and walking are ideal, but be guided by your doctor.

If you think that you are at risk of a heart attack, discuss with your GP the possibility of taking steps to monitor and treat this.

Some heart conditions can be controlled by drugs, which your GP will advise you about. For long-term treatment, various heart operations are now common.

For more information, contact the British Heart Foundation at the address on page 192.

High blood pressure

Blood pressure is the force that keeps the blood circulating round the body. People with high blood pressure (hypertension) may feel perfectly well and experience no symptoms, but statistics show that they are far more likely to develop certain vascular diseases – such as stroke, heart attack or kidney failure – than people with lower blood pressure. These risks are reduced if the blood pressure is lowered.

The Stroke Association (address on page 194) produces a wide range of information to help prevent stroke or assist in recovering from stroke. Its leaflet, *Stroke: questions and answers*, is available in five different Asian languages, as Asian people are particularly at risk of stroke.

Most people with high blood pressure need to take some form of medication. However, there are certain things you can do yourself to help lower blood pressure:

- Lose weight if you are overweight.
- Eat less salt.
- Give up smoking and limit your alcohol intake.
- Avoid stress.
- Consult your doctor about whether exercise might help.

Blood pressure should be checked every year – if you have not had your blood pressure measured recently, ask for this to be done by your GP or practice nurse.

Incontinence

Although incontinence is common among older people, it is not a 'normal' part of ageing. Many types of incontinence can be treated or cured. That is why it is so important to overcome the inhibitions some people feel about talking about such personal matters, and find out why you, or the person you are caring for, has a problem.

Stress incontinence – leaking of urine when you laugh, cough or sneeze – is mainly experienced by women. It can be caused by stretching of the pelvic floor muscles during childbirth or by hormonal changes following the menopause. This can be cured completely and quickly by exercises to strengthen the pelvic muscles.

To feel your pelvic muscles, imagine you are trying to control diarrhoea by tightening the muscles round the back passage. Then imagine you are trying to stop passing urine by tightening the muscles around the outlet from the bladder. Slowly tighten the pelvic muscles, working back to front, to a slow count of four, then gently let go. Repeat four times. These exercises can be done sitting, standing or lying down. You should do them at least four times a day: the more often, the sooner you will feel the benefit.

Frequency or urgency – needing to pass urine very frequently or experiencing a sudden strong urge to do so – may be caused by an infection or other problems, so consult your doctor. Bladder training may help: when you want to pass urine urgently, practise holding on, first for a minute, then gradually for longer.

Leaking or dribbling is more common in men and is often caused by prostate problems. It can also be caused by constipation, which can create pressure on the bladder. Consult your doctor if you are experiencing this problem.

Whatever form of incontinence you suffer from, it is important to keep as active as possible, eat lots of fibre and drink plenty (two litres every 24 hours). This will help prevent constipation, which can lead to both bladder and bowel problems.

It is also worth making sure that you, or the person you are caring for, go to the toilet regularly. If you have an older relative in a care home who suffers from incontinence, you should check that there are enough toilets, that people are helped to go to the toilet at regular intervals, and that clothing can be unfastened easily.

If incontinence is to be successfully treated, the first step is accurate diagnosis. Always consult your doctor. He or she should be able to help, but there may also be a specially trained continence adviser in your area – check with your GP or health visitor. The continence adviser should be able to identify the cause of incontinence and suggest appropriate treatment, whether in the form of exercise, medication or other treatments. He or she will also be able to give advice on the wide range of products and equipment available to help cope with incontinence, some of which may be obtainable free on the NHS.

For more information and advice, contact the Continence Foundation at the address on page 192. Age Concern Factsheet 23 is called *Help with continence*.

Osteoporosis

Osteoporosis is thinning and weakening of the bones. Thousands of older women suffer painful and deforming fractures – of hips, wrists and spine – and men can be affected too.

After the menopause, as the oestrogen level in women's bodies declines, women begin to lose bone from their skeleton, sometimes gradually and sometimes very rapidly. Those particularly at risk include:

- women who have had an early menopause or hysterectomy;
- women who have over-dieted or suffered anorexia or bulimia nervosa, as their calcium intake may have been very low;
- women who have over-exercised or who have missed a lot of periods for other reasons;
- men or women who have already had a fracture after a minor fall or who have already lost height;
- those who have had to take corticosteroids for some time; and
- heavy smokers or drinkers.

Research has shown that there is a lot you can do to keep your bones strong and healthy:

Weight-bearing exercise such as walking, dancing or keep fit makes bones stronger and also improves balance and coordination, which makes falling less likely.

Calcium in the diet is vital. Cheese, yoghurt and milk are the best sources – skimmed milk is even better than full fat.

Giving up smoking and drinking alcohol will help: smoking lowers oestrogen levels and alcohol prevents calcium being absorbed.

Hormone Replacement Therapy (HRT) replaces the oestrogen lost after the menopause. It is available in the form of pills, patches and implants. HRT provides protection against bone loss during the period while you are actually having it. As bone loss occurs at the highest rate immediately after the menopause, having HRT for five or ten years at this time can reduce the risk of fractures in later life by as much as 60 per cent. It also significantly reduces the risk of heart disease. However, HRT is not suitable for everyone: it is thought that long-term use may increase the risk of breast cancer, but research continues in this area.

These preventative measures may benefit people who already suffer from osteoporosis and help prevent further bone loss. Drugs and calcium tablets may also be prescribed. Specialist osteoporosis centres may offer treatments that are not yet available on general prescription.

Physiotherapy may be useful both for pain relief and to increase mobility and help regain muscle strength after a fracture.

For more information about the causes, prevention and treatment of osteoporosis, including HRT, contact the National Osteoporosis Society at the address on page 193.

For more information about health, see the Age Concern Books publications *Better Health in Retirement* and *Know your Complementary Therapies* (details on page 201).

Help with health costs

Most of the treatment given under the NHS is free – for example, **hearing services** (see page 141) and **chiropody services** (see page 136) are free under the NHS. There are some things, however, for which most people have to pay part or all of the cost.

If you or your partner receive Income Support, income-based Jobseeker's Allowance or Disabled Persons Tax Credit (depending on the level of your award), you can receive help with some health costs. If you do not receive any of these benefits but your savings are no more than £12,000 (£8,000 if you are under 60), you can apply for help with health costs under the NHS Low Income Scheme. Certificate HC 2 entitles you to full help, while certificate HC 3 entitles you to more limited help. To apply, get form HC 1 from your local social security office or NHS hospital; some dentists, opticians and GP surgeries also have them. If you get Income Support, you do not need to apply for a certificate but can simply show your order book or a letter from the social security office.

Prescriptions are free if you are aged 60 or over. They are also free to younger people if they have a low income.

Dental care, including checkups and dentures, are free if you or your partner gets Income Support or you have certificate HC 2. The cost may be reduced if you have certificate HC 3. If you are not entitled to help, you will have to pay 80 per cent of the cost of most treatment (see page 134).

Sight tests are free to all people aged 60 or over. Younger people will also qualify if they or their partner receives Income Support or has certificate HC 2.

Vouchers towards the cost of **glasses** are available if you or your partner gets Income Support or has certificate HC 2. You may get some help if you have certificate HC 3. Help with **hospital travel costs** is available too for those on Income Support and may be available for those with certificate HC 2 or HC 3.

If you are aged 65 or over you should be offered free flu vaccinations.

Copies of *Your guide to the NHS*, as well as a range of publications on various health issues, are available from NHS Direct at the address on page 193.

Ageing Well (address on page 191) has a leaflet called *You and your doctor ... working together.*

Relationships

Our relationships are an important part of our lives whatever age we are. Retirement is a time of change and can affect all of your relationships.

This chapter looks at sex in later life, at what support is available if you are a carer, and at coping with bereavement.

- ● **Sex in later life**
- ● **Bereavement**
- ● **Caring for someone**

Sex in later life

It is all too easy to get the impression from the media that sex is only for the young and beautiful – beauty being identified with being slim, lithe and unwrinkled. Even in this frank age, it still surprises and even shocks younger people that their elders are sexually interested and active. Yet many couples in fact enjoy sex more as they get older, finding this aspect of their lives rewarding and fulfilling and just as important to them as to younger couples.

Normal ageing changes, whether social, psychological or physical, affect performance less than is sometimes thought. Sexual behaviour varies considerably over time among couples of all ages. Sometimes sex is passionate, sometimes it is calmer and quieter. At times it may become less important or even burdensome – desire can be affected by a range of factors, from physical health and emotional well-being to worries about family, work or money.

Most people are able to enjoy some form of sexual love throughout their lives, but our sexuality may not always be expressed in the same way. For some older people, orgasm may become less frequent and less intense; the shared intimacy of body contact, the lying next to each other, of stroking, touching, caressing and being held, may become more important than actual intercourse.

Growing older may in fact bring some very real advantages as far as our sexual lives are concerned:

- Once women are past the menopause, they and their partners can enjoy intercourse without fear of an unwanted pregnancy. (However, there is the risk of HIV infection for people having intercourse with a new partner without using a condom.)
- For many women the fact that their partner now takes longer to reach a climax makes sex far more enjoyable than before.
- When people retire they may have more time and energy for sex and sexual exploration and find that their sex lives actually improve.

Improving your sex life

For some older couples sexual intercourse becomes increasingly infrequent; eventually they give it up entirely. Often the main reason is boredom: the same thing done in the same way at the same time in the same place tends to become boring for anyone. Women were often not taught to expect any pleasure from sex; as a result many have never enjoyed it and may be relieved to give it up altogether. Men may be unimaginative about intercourse, partly because they too expect women to be passive and unresponsive.

Anyone who harbours even the slightest feeling that older people should not really have sexual desires may feel uneasy, even guilty, at the idea of sexual exploration. This may be even more the case for people who are attracted to people of their own sex. This is a pity because there are many ways in which people, young and old, whatever their sexual orientation, can attempt to improve their sex lives.

Talking about what you want

Most of us find it hard to talk about sex, even to our partners of many years' standing. Yet the fact that someone cares for us does not mean that they will automatically know what we want and when, what we like and don't like. If partners are expected to guess, it is not surprising that they sometimes guess wrong. Learning to communicate what we want, either in words or by our actions, and in turn becoming more attuned to our partner's needs, can improve and enrich our love lives immensely.

Trying something new

Many couples have only used one or two positions for intercourse – most common for heterosexuals is probably the missionary position, in which the man lies on top of the woman – but trying different positions can in itself produce new sensations.

Perhaps one of the problems is that many couples regard sex as an almost entirely genital activity. Yet people often like to spend time kissing and caressing before any genital contact is made, and some may prefer non-penetrative sex or enjoy a great deal of manual stimulation of the genitals before intercourse – some women may only reach orgasm this way.

Some couples might feel curious about oral sex but feel inhibited about trying it. The fact that it is sometimes regarded as almost a perversion may make it harder to accept that it is perfectly normal.

The same is true of sex aids such as vibrators and dildos. Until recently often considered as unnatural, they too can enhance lovemaking and help partners give each other maximum satisfaction. Watching explicit movies together can also be stimulating and arouse sexual feelings. Anyone, regardless of age, should feel free to try anything that they and their partner feel happy about.

A complete change of scene can also be exciting – going to bed and making love during the day, making love in a different room in the house. One of the bonuses of retirement is that this is so much more possible. Having a special supper together – either at home or in a restaurant – can reintroduce the romantic element that may have disappeared from our lives. Watching a film or having a bath together can be a good prelude to going to bed. Finally, a short trip away from home can give a couple an opportunity to rediscover their enjoyment of each other.

Sensate focusing

Sensate focusing is a form of sex therapy; it was pioneered by Masters and Johnson in the United States and is sometimes known by their names. It is particularly suitable for couples who are having arousal problems, such as frigidity, impotence or an inability to enjoy sex, in that it concentrates on each partner giving and receiving pleasure rather than worrying about sexual intercourse.

The treatment consists of three separate phases, which may last several weeks each. During the first phase, the couple are told to stroke each other's bodies, apart from the genitals, telling each other what they like and don't like. At this stage most therapists recommend that there should be no sexual intercourse, however much the couple desire it. At the next stage genital stimulation is also allowed, with the couple again telling each other what they like and don't like. Finally, they go on to full intercourse.

For information about the availability of sexual and marital therapy, in both NHS and private sectors, send an sae to the British Association for Sexual and Marital Therapy at the address on page 194.

Sexual problems

Sexual problems can occur for many reasons – because of a medical condition; after an operation; because of the circumstances in which a couple live; or for reasons that are more explicitly sexual, such as anxiety about performance.

Couples sometimes stop having sex altogether because of a specific difficulty, which they may attribute to ageing. But such difficulties can usually be overcome and sexual activity resumed.

Arthritis can make sex painful. Arthritis of the hip in particular can make it difficult for a woman to open her legs, making intercourse with a woman lying on her back impossible. One solution is for the woman to lie on her side, with the man lying behind her 'like a pair of spoons'. The use of pillows to support painful limbs may be helpful, as may an extra dose of painkillers, preferably before foreplay begins. (See pages 137–138 for more about arthritis.)

Drugs can affect sexual performance and enjoyment. If this is reported to the doctor, the treatment can sometimes be changed. Doctors should always tell patients of possible side-effects so that they can make an informed choice about their own treatment.

Incontinence affects many older people (see pages 143–144) and can be embarrassing if it occurs during intercourse. One solution is to empty the bladder immediately before starting to make love and to avoid drinking in the two or three hours before bedtime.

Breathlessness or disability from a heart attack or a stroke may all make it necessary to use techniques that reduce the effort involved: lovemaking should be as gentle and undemanding as possible. The affected partner should avoid taking too active a role, and might try being propped up in bed or sitting up on a chair rather than lying flat. Non-penetrative sex might sometimes be better than full intercourse.

Depression often causes loss of sexual desire. Although many people see this as a symptom of ageing, it is actually an illness that can be cured, by drugs or counselling or a mixture of the two.

Operations can leave people feeling very low, and they are often afraid that sex will be harmful. Patients and their partners should be fully informed about what to expect before the operation, and offered help with any difficulties afterwards, including advice as to when it is safe to resume sexual activity. Prostate operations for men, and mastectomy and hysterectomy operations for women, may be particularly traumatic. There are specially trained nurses who help people who have had a colostomy operation.

Vaginal dryness and tightness may be a problem for some women after the menopause. This can be overcome by the use of a lubricant such as KY Jelly or any contraceptive cream, and in the longer term possibly by hormone replacement therapy (HRT – see page 145).

Sexual performance is a problem for many men. Total or partial impotence (when the penis doesn't become hard enough for intercourse) can be caused by a physical disease, by the fact that older men have less of the hormone testosterone than when they were younger, or by anxiety about performing satisfactorily. Problems can be helped by counselling and sensate focusing, or by the use of penile rings (available from sex shops and some chemists), injections or, very occasionally, surgical treatment.

More recently, the drug Viagra has become available for the treatment of impotence. It can be prescribed by a GP in some circumstances but patients are usually referred to a consultant urologist or specialist, who can assess which type of treatment, including Viagra, might be suitable. Care has to be taken when someone has angina or has had a heart attack in the past.

General problems within a relationship can also cause sexual difficulties. The reality of retirement may not match up to expectations, and couples may find it difficult to adjust to suddenly having so much more time together. Good retirement courses can help a couple talk about their hopes and fears. Couples who need help in working through their problems could see a counsellor. Counsellors may be attached to doctors' surgeries, or you may be able to see one through Relate.

For the address of your nearest Relate branch, either look in your local phone book or contact Relate at the address on page 196.

The Association to Aid the Sexual and Personal Relationships of People with a Disability (SPOD) – address on page 196 – provides an advisory and counselling service for people with disabilities who are having sexual difficulties.

People on their own

Factfile

- In 2000, 19 per cent of men and 37 per cent of women in the 65–74 age group lived alone; 33 per cent of men and 60 per cent of women aged 75 and over lived alone.

- In 2000, 76 per cent of men in the 65–74 age group were married, compared to 56 per cent of women.

Although having a partner is by no means an automatic solution to all life's problems, there are certain things it does make easier. You have someone to go on holiday with, to go to the cinema with, to share both your major worries and your day-to-day experiences. You also have some-one – potentially at least – to satisfy your sexual needs.

Many people were brought up to regard masturbation as sinful and some still feel guilty about it. Yet everyone has some sexual needs, and satisfying those needs is just one more thing that people on their own have to do for themselves. Many single people find the use of a sex aid such as a vibrator helpful.

Finding a new partner

Many people on their own hope that they will find a new partner. This is particularly difficult for older women: not only are they far more numer-ous than older men, but men of their own age may be looking for much younger partners. Older men, on the other hand, find themselves out-numbered by women almost everywhere they go.

Many people find that the opportunities for meeting new people are few and far between, especially once they have left work and their children have left home. Starting new activities outside the home – joining a club or society, going to an evening class, doing some voluntary work – can all help. Another option is to go to a dating agency or a marriage bureau.

People go to marriage bureaux for many different reasons. Some want a long-term relationship – someone to live with or marry. Others seek only companionship and a friend to see two or three times a week, and perhaps go on holiday with. For some people, sex will be an important part of any relationship; for others, it will be less important or even unwanted. Anyone who goes to a marriage bureau should be as clear as possible about what they want and what they do not want. They should also try to find out from the people they meet through the bureau what they want from the relationship.

When we talk about sexual experience and finding a new partner, we tend to think of love between a man and a woman, but it could also be love between two people of the same sex. Many people are capable of both heterosexual and homosexual love: someone who was happily married for years may find that a close friendship with someone of their own sex can include warmth and physical affection, and even extend to a sexual relationship.

Bereavement

The death of someone we love deeply is probably the most devastating experience that will ever happen to us. People have described it as feeling like 'being cut in half'. In addition to these overwhelming emotions, our lives may seem to be thrown into turmoil, with both our day-to-day routine and our hopes and plans for the future completely overturned. This section looks at both the process of grieving itself and the practical arrangements that need to be made immediately after a death.

Coping with grief

Mourning is essential to our well-being and our recovery. We need to allow ourselves time to mourn: blocking our feelings only delays the process of healing. Eventually we will reach a time when it becomes possible to start to rebuild our lives.

The stages of grief

Although each person's reaction to bereavement is unique, grief does usually have an overall pattern. Most of us will go through the stages of shock and disbelief, intense sadness and pain, regrets, longing, depression, perhaps anger, aggression and guilt. We do not all experience all these feelings, nor do we experience them in the same order or with the same intensity. It may nevertheless be reassuring to know that these feelings are shared by many others and that they will not last forever.

Shock and disbelief are usually the first reactions. You may feel numb and unreal, especially if the death has been sudden and unexpected. The reality of the funeral can help you begin to accept that the person you love has died.

Feelings of loss can at times be so overwhelming that you may almost feel you are breaking down or going mad. Symptoms such as loss of appetite, sleeplessness, exhaustion, restlessness and feelings of panic are all common. It is important to try to eat sensibly and generally look after yourself, however little you may feel like it.

Anger and aggression can also be expressions of grief. Death can seem cruel and unfair, especially if the person has died young. You may rail against God or fate, against those responsible for the death, against yourself for being unable to prevent it, against the person who has died for leaving you in the lurch. You may feel resentful towards other people who have not experienced a loss – 'why did this happen to me and not them?'

Feelings of guilt are also common, and can be very destructive. You may hold yourself partly to blame for the death: 'if only I had called the doctor sooner'. Things left undone and unsaid may loom very large in your mind.

Depression, despair and apathy will probably at some stage beset anyone who has lost someone they love. Life without them may seem pointless, and getting through each day may be a struggle. But if the depression never seems to lift, you should see your doctor: you might be suffering from clinical depression, which can be treated.

Remembering and reliving the past is part of grieving. Although this may at first be painful, it can bring back happy memories, which can be very comforting.

Some people find it easier to show their feelings than others, but most find at some stage that it helps to talk – whether to family friends, your local priest or a trained bereavement counsellor.

Signs of recovery

When you first suffer a bereavement, it seems almost impossible to imagine that the pain will ever get any less, that you will ever again be without a lump in your throat and a knot in your stomach. Then after a time – and no one can dictate how long that time should be – you realise that a few hours have passed and you haven't thought of the person you have lost. You may at first feel guilty about this: it seems almost a betrayal that you can forget in this way. But don't feel guilty: this is the beginning of recovery. You are gradually accepting the reality that the person you loved is gone, that they are part of your past and that you will still have a life ahead of you to be lived.

There will of course be ups and downs, and periods when things seem to be getting worse not better. At first you may well find family occasions and festivals, such as anniversaries and Christmas and New Year, particularly sad. Setbacks like this are inevitable, but slowly and surely the process of healing will go on.

If the person who has died is your partner of many years, one long-term effect is loneliness. You may miss their physical presence, the intimacy, and having someone always on hand to talk to and do things with. Living alone may seem almost unbearable, and the effort required to build up a new life impossibly great. If it is the person who you have been caring for who has died, there may be additional complicating factors, such as a powerful feeling of relief, which may shock you.

There may be a local bereavement counselling service in the area. Contact your local Age Concern or library for information. Cruse Bereavement Care has volunteer counsellors all over the country who can talk on the telephone, answer letters or visit people at home. Local branches also organise regular social meetings for bereaved people.

 For more information, contact Cruse at the address on page 195.

Practical arrangements to be made after a death

When someone we love dies we may feel we just want to crawl away and hide like a wounded animal, but we usually have to face all sorts of practical problems. Not knowing what to do about the formalities can add to the distress. The immediate tasks are registering the death and arranging the funeral. In addition, the dead person's will (if there is one) may have to be 'proved', and their property disposed of in accordance with it.

Registering the death

If the death occurs at home, the family doctor who looked after the person in their last illness will give a death certificate. This must be taken to the Registrar of Births and Deaths for the area within five days of the death. It is also possible to make a formal declaration giving all the necessary information in any other register office, which will be passed on to the registrar for the area in which the death occurred. This may be helpful if you are trying to make arrangements from some distance away.

The doctor should be able to tell you where the office is, or you can look in the phone book or ask at the Citizens Advice Bureau.

If the death occurs in hospital, you still have to take the death certificate to the registrar's office, but it will be the office for the hospital area, not for the person's home. The hospital staff will be able to tell where this is when you collect the certificate. It is also possible to register the death at any register office, as described above.

The hospital doctors may want to perform a post-mortem examination on the dead person's body; in this case the closest relative will be asked for their consent. Sometimes too the routines are delayed because the death has to be referred to the coroner, perhaps because the death was sudden or unexpected. The coroner will then decide whether it is necessary to hold a post mortem.

In addition to the date and place of death, the registrar will need to know the full names of the person who has died (including the maiden surname of a woman who has been married), their date and place of birth, their most recent occupation and their spouse's full name and occupation. Once the register is signed, the registrar will issue you with:

- A certificate of disposal (green), which allows burial or cremation to go ahead and which is to be given to the funeral director.
- A certificate of registration (white), which contains a social security form to claim any remaining benefit due to the dead person's estate.
- The death certificate, which costs £3.50 (in 2002). Further copies of the death certificate can be purchased if needed, for example to arrange probate and close a bank account or other accounts.

For more information, see social security leaflet D49 *What to do after a death.*

Arranging the funeral

If you are arranging a funeral, always check whether the dead person left any instructions about the funeral, or had taken out funeral insurance (see page 47).

If you do not have the means to pay for even a simple funeral, and there is insufficient money in the dead person's estate, you may qualify for a Funeral Payment from the Social Fund (see page 22).

Always get a written, itemised estimate of all the costs involved – funeral directors accept that relatives may wish to get several quotations before deciding which company to use.

 The National Association of Funeral Directors (address on page 195) has a code of practice for its members. It also operates a complaints procedure.

The funeral director can arrange for the body to be taken to a chapel of rest once the death has been certified. They must have the burial or cremation certificates before the funeral can take place.

Everyone has the right to a church funeral, but it is not necessary to have a service at a funeral, whether it is a burial or a cremation; a relative or friend can say a few words, or a non-religious ceremony can be held.

 For advice and help with a non-religious ceremony, contact the British Humanist Association at the address on page 194.

Everyone has the right to burial in the churchyard of the parish in which they die – provided there is one and there is space in it. An alternative is to be buried in a cemetery. These are usually run by the local authority. Information about fees and rules can be obtained by writing for brochures.

For more information about all aspects of arranging a funeral, see Age Concern Factsheet 27 *Arranging a funeral*. As Scottish law is different from English law, a Scottish version of the factsheet is also available from Freephone 0800 00 99 66.

Dealing with probate

When a person dies their assets may be frozen until probate is granted. No one – not even a spouse – will be able to draw money from their bank account (unless it is a joint account).

The personal representative

The responsibility for obtaining probate falls to the 'personal representative' of the person who has died. If appointed by the will, they are called an executor (male) or an executrix (female). If there was no will, or no executor named, then the personal representative is called an administrator (male) or an administratrix (female). The person appointed is usually the next of kin or the main beneficiary of the will.

If the estate is complicated or the will is likely to be contested, the personal representative should consider using a solicitor. The personal representative can deduct his or her expenses from the estate, but only a professional executor can be paid for the work involved in dealing with the estate.

The grant of representation

The personal representative needs a formal legal document from the High Court to confirm that they have the legal authority to deal with the assets of the dead person. In effect, a grant of representation transfers all the money and property of the person who has died to the personal representative, to distribute according to the instructions set out in the will or according to the intestacy rules (explained on page 46). The document is called a 'grant of probate' when issued to executors who are said to have 'proved' the will. An administrator is given a grant of letters of administration.

The procedure is the same whether you are applying for a grant of probate or letters of administration. The local probate registry (the address of which can be obtained from your local library or telephone directory) provides the forms and a leaflet called *How to obtain probate* (PA2), which tells you how to complete the relevant application forms. As personal representative you will have to complete several forms:

■ **The Probate Application (Form PA1)** This asks for details abut the person who has died, their surviving relatives, the personal representative, and the will if there is one.

■ **A Return of the Whole Estate (Form IHT 205)** (yellow form) This asks for details of the estate and its value and is used to prepare the account for the Inland Revenue, as Inheritance Tax may have to be paid. If the value is over £220,000, then use **Form IHT 200**, which is available from the Capital Taxes Office. Do not fill in both forms.

In order to complete the necessary forms you will have to obtain information on:

■ the value at the date of death of all assets owned by the dead person;
■ any money owed to the dead person; and
■ any debts owed by the dead person, including tax.

The completed forms, together with the death certificate and the original will (or any documents in which the deceased person expresses any wishes about the distribution of their estate), should be sent to the probate registry office in the area where you want to be interviewed. Send the documents by recorded delivery after making a copy of them.

Once the probate registry has prepared all the legal documents, you will be asked to come for an interview, to confirm the details you have given. You will have to pay a standard fee of £130 (no fee is payable, however, if the net estate is worth £5,000 or less). You may also order extra official copies of the grant of representation to send to institutions holding assets of the dead person – an ordinary photocopy is not usually acceptable.

When a grant may not be needed

A grant of representation may not be needed if:

■ All the property in the estate is owned in joint names as joint tenants; this means the property automatically becomes wholly owned by the surviving joint tenant.

- All assets are held in joint names.
- The total amount of savings is less than £5,000.
- The estate is made up entirely of cash (bank notes and coins) and personal possessions.
- A 'nomination agreement' exists (these could only be made before 1981).

To find out whether the assets can be obtained without a grant, you have to write to each institution informing them of the death and enclosing a copy of the death certificate (a photocopy of the will should also be enclosed if there is one) and details of the assets and your relationship to the deceased.

Paying Inheritance Tax

You usually have to pay Inheritance Tax (if it is due – see page 33) before probate/administration is granted, but it is not always possible to use money from the estate to pay it until you have the grant of representation. You may therefore need to raise money to pay both Inheritance Tax and probate fees.

You may be able to obtain the funds from money held by the dead person in National Savings investments or Government stocks, or from a bank or building society account, if the institution concerned agrees.

It is advisable at the outset to open a separate bank or building society account, known as an 'executorship account', to which all money paid into the estate can be credited. If this is done, the bank or building society will often agree to lend the money to pay the tax and probate fees, provided that the estate is of sufficient value to cover the loan.

Settling the estate

Once all the application procedures have been completed, and Inheritance Tax and probate fees paid, the grant of representation will be issued in the form of the probate/administration document.

You can now begin to settle the estate and arrange for the distribution of property and possessions. You will need to do the following:

- Obtain all the assets belonging to the estate, sending an official copy of the grant to each institution holding assets. The institution should return the document after registering the particulars in their records.
- Advertise formally for creditors, if the personal representative is not also the main beneficiary.
- Pay the outstanding debts of the estate – if there seems to be insufficient money to pay all the debts, seek legal advice.
- Finalise the payment of taxes.
- Distribute the estate either according to the terms of the will or under the intestacy rules if there is no will.

When distributing the assets, you should obtain a signed receipt from each beneficiary. Once all specific bequests have been made, you should prepare estate accounts. The residue or remainder of the estate can then be transferred to the main beneficiary.

For more information, see Age Concern Factsheet 14 *Dealing with someone's estate.* As Scottish law is different from English law, a Scottish version of the factsheet is available from Freephone 0800 00 99 66.

Caring for someone

If you have a parent or other older relative who is finding it difficult to cope, you may find yourself in the position of having to make arrangements to enable them to manage. One option is for them to move in with you or other relatives. Another option is to make use of the support services that are available to enable them to stay in their own home, if necessary adapting the home to make it more convenient and easy to manage. If more day-to-day care is needed, then a care home might be considered. This section looks at the different options and also at support for carers.

Living with relatives or friends

If you are thinking of having an older relative or friend to live with you, you should always weigh up the pros and cons carefully. It is all too easy to enter into such arrangements without either party realising how much their independence may be affected. These are some of the points that are worth considering:

- Is your home conveniently situated for shops, transport and other facilities? It will probably not suit you or your relative if you find yourself having to drive them everywhere they want to go.
- Where will their room be? Unless they have a downstairs room, there is always the risk that they may come to find the stairs difficult and end up staying longer in their room than they want to, or staying downstairs longer than they want to, once they have got down.
- Is there a good-sized spare room, so that you and they will be able to invite friends to stay?
- If you have children at home, or you help to look after grandchildren, will your relative find living with them too much, however fond of the children they are?
- What are the arrangements for washing, cleaning and other chores?
- What happens if your relative starts to need more day-to-day care? They may be totally independent at first, but this could change. If you have discussed these possibilities before they move in, at least you will have gone into the arrangement with your eyes open.

Having a parent or other older relative living in a self-contained 'granny flat' or annexe linked to your home can be an ideal arrangement and this type of arrangement would normally be considered as self-contained accommodation. Problems can arise, however – the crucial thing is that you should both have similar expectations about how much time you are going to spend together, how much time they are going to spend looking after their grandchildren, and so on.

If your relative is receiving social security benefits such as Income Support or Attendance Allowance, they are likely to go on receiving them if they move in with you. However, they will not be able to receive Housing Benefit towards any rent they pay you unless they live separately, either in a 'granny flat' or in the same house but only sharing areas such as hall and bathroom.

Legal arrangements

However good an arrangement seems, circumstances can change, or you may simply not get on as well as you had hoped. If an older relative puts money into buying a property with you, or into improvements or adaptations to your existing home, they probably should have a legal share in the property. Be aware, however, that this could pose serious problems for you if they ever have to go into a care home.

See Age Concern Factsheet 38 *Treatment of the former home as capital for people in care homes* for information about how the value of your property is treated if other people are living there.

On the other hand, you may want to have an agreement that enables you to ask them to leave if certain conditions are breached. For example, the agreement might prevent them bringing any other person to live in your home without your permission. You will also want to talk to your solicitor about ownership of your home – in most circumstances it would seem sensible for you to remain the sole owner. Think about all the points mentioned above, so that whatever happens you can both turn to the legal agreement to sort things out as fairly as possible.

Adapting the home

If your parent or relative has a particular disability or medical condition and has difficulty moving around, or with routine domestic tasks such as making a cup of tea, there are a lot of simple, straightforward things that can be done to make life easier.

Mobility aids A walking stick, walking frame, rollator (wheeled frame) or wheelchair might make it easier to move around. All these mobility aids can be obtained free. The hospital, physiotherapy or occupational therapy department or the local social services department can give advice.

Layout of the house Are doors easy to open, and wide enough for someone using a wheelchair or walking frame? Are parts of the house so cluttered it is difficult to move around? If the stairs are a problem, grab rails or banisters could be fitted on both sides. Obvious hazards, such as trailing flexes, loose floor coverings or slippery floors, can be removed.

Furniture If a person has difficulty getting up from a low chair or bed, a more suitable one could be bought – the Disabled Living Foundation can give you advice on this. Repositioning furniture can also help – for example, putting a chair or stool in the bathroom to sit on while drying and dressing.

Bathroom and toilet Securely fixed grab rails and poles can make it much easier to get in and out of the bath or on and off the toilet. Slip-resistant flooring, and a slip-resistant mat in the shower or bath, will reduce the risk of falling. Doors should always open outwards so that if someone falls behind the door it will be easy to reach them.

Kitchen If this is separate from the dining room, a trolley or a hatch between the rooms might be helpful. Being able to sit down to do certain tasks makes preparing meals less tiring. Units should be easily accessible and within reach. For someone with arthritic hands, there are a number of gadgets available, for example to help with opening tins and jars.

Help and advice

Occupational therapists (OTs) can give detailed advice. OTs assess a person's ability to move around and carry out daily tasks and suggest aids and adaptations to overcome any difficulties. Contact the local social service department and ask for an assessment of needs. The social services authority may be able to provide some aids or equipment free if a person is assessed as needing them.

For more information about special equipment and furniture, contact the Disabled Living Foundation at the address on page 195.

Age Concern Factsheet 42 *Disability equipment and how to get it* provides other useful contacts and publications.

For information about financial help with alterations, see pages 112–114.

Community care services

Whether someone needs a couple of hours' help a week – perhaps with shopping – or daily nursing care, being able to get the help they need at home can make all the difference. If your relative is having difficulty coping at home, get in touch with the local authority social services department, or the family doctor, to see if they can offer advice or support.

If your relative feels that they need help to remain at home, they can ask the local authority for an assessment of their needs. The social services department will be responsible for arranging the assessment, although, under the new Single Assessment Process for Older People, it may be done on behalf of social services by someone from another organisation such as a care trust.

Since April 2001, you, as a carer, are also entitled to an assessment in your own right and to services that will help you care for them. You have a right to an assessment even if your relative does not want to be assessed.

For further information, see Age Concern Factsheet 41 *Local authority assessments for community care services*.

Each social services department offers different kinds of help and support and has its own criteria for deciding how much, if anything, people have to pay. Some services are provided directly by social services and others may be provided on their behalf by another organisation, such as a charity or private agency. Another alternative is a direct payment, where you are provided with funds to buy your own care.

Some of the most common services that may be available for older people and people with disabilities are:

- **Equipment and adaptations** (see pages 168–169).
- **Alarm systems** (see pages 108–109).
- **Day care** outside a person's home. Some day centres offer specialist care, for example for people with dementia; others offer mainly a chance to meet other people and share activities and a meal.
- **Home help or home care assistant** – such care may be provided through organisations such as local Age Concerns or Crossroads – Caring for Carers organisations (see address on page 195). Some people make their own private arrangements.
- **Laundry services** for people with incontinence or other problems.
- **Home meal services** – some are run by Age Concern locally or WRVS organisations (see national address on page 196) for local authorities.
- **Respite care** which gives the carer and the person being cared for a break from each other – for a few hours, a day, a night, a week or two weeks. A new system of vouchers is due to be introduced. 'Sitting' schemes also enable carers to take a break, either regularly or in emergencies.
- **Transport schemes** (eg dial-a-ride) (see page 78).

 Age Concern Factsheet 20 *NHS continuing care, free nursing care and intermediate care* explains about respite care from the NHS. For more information about respite care, contact Carers UK at the address on page 195.

See also Age Concern Factsheet 32 *Disability and ageing: your rights to social services* and Factsheet 46 *Paying for help at home and local authority charges.*

The family doctor should be able you put you in touch with community health services. These may include:

- **District nurses** or **health visitors**
- **Chiropody and nail-cutting services** (see pages 135–136)
- **Continence advice** (see pages 143–144)
- **Physiotherapy**
- **Community mental health nurses**

For more information, see Age Concern Factsheet 44 *Community health services.*

For information about seeking companions or live-in help, see Factsheet 6 *Finding help at home.*

Moving to a care home

Only a small minority of older people move to a care home, but if your relative needs a high degree of personal care, they may consider such a move. When choosing a home, it is advisable to look at more than one if possible. Have a good look round and talk to the staff and residents. Some of the questions it might be worth asking include:

- How much choice does the home offer residents about aspects of everyday life such as what and when they eat, when and where they see visitors and when they get up and go to bed?
- Do residents have the choice of single or shared rooms? If rooms are shared, can they choose who they share with?
- Can residents bring any personal possessions with them, such as pictures, plants or furniture?
- Do residents have the use of a telephone in privacy?
- Is there more than one living room; a quiet one as well as one with a television? Are there smoking and non-smoking rooms?
- Can wheelchairs go everywhere in the home? Is there a lift?
- Does the home arrange to take residents out to the shops, to the theatre and other entertainment and to places of worship?
- Is there a residents' committee?
- Does the home encourage residents to make comments or complaints about the home?
- What is included in the fee and what counts as an 'extra'?

The home must publish a brochure outlining what it provides, the philosophy of the home, and the fees it charges. Make sure that the reality of the home matches the brochure – it is always a good idea for a prospective resident to have a trial stay before making a final decision.

 Age Concern Factsheet 29 *Finding care home accommodation* includes a list of organisations that provide information and advice.

Paying for care homes

People who can find and afford to pay for a home for themselves can claim, or continue to claim, Attendance Allowance (AA) or Disability Living Allowance (DLA) provided they fulfil the other conditions (see page 26). If their money subsequently runs low, they can apply to the local authority, as explained below. If financially supported by the local authority, they will stop receiving AA/DLA after four weeks.

People who need care in a care home but cannot afford it have to approach the local authority for an assessment of their needs (as described on page 169 above). If the local authority agrees to place them in a home, it pays the cost of the place but collects a charge from the resident based on national rules for assessment of capital and income.

Residents with savings and capital (including property) of more than £19,000 (18,500 in Scotland) have to pay the full cost of the fees themselves (but in certain circumstances the value of their home will be ignored). Those with £19,000 or less have their income and savings assessed to see how much they have to pay themselves. If someone wishes to live in a more expensive home than the local authority is willing to pay for, they must pay the extra fees through a third party.

Those with £16,000 or less may be able to receive Income Support as well as financial support from the local authority towards the fees. The value of the home will normally be taken into account.

For more information about the system for people needing local authority support, see Age Concern Factsheet 10 *Local authority charging procedures for care homes*.

People who need nursing care may have their care arranged and fully paid for by the health authority if they meet the local criteria for continuing health care services. The NHS is also now responsible for the funding of care provided by a registered nurse in a care home providing nursing care for all those who fund their own care – this part of the care is thus free.

 For more information, see Age Concern Factsheet 20 *NHS continuing care, free nursing care and intermediate care*.

When one of a couple enters a care home, the local authority will assess how much the resident must pay towards the fees solely on the resident's savings and income. However, the spouse is regarded as a 'liable relative' and may be asked to contribute towards the cost.

If a resident has an occupational or personal pension and a spouse living at home, the local authority will ignore half the pension when assessing the resident's income provided that they pass at least this amount to their spouse.

 For more information, see Age Concern Factsheet 39 *Paying for care in a care home if you have a partner*.

Support for carers

Caring for someone over a long period of time can affect the health of the carer. Irritability, headaches, constant tiredness, loss of appetite, depression or tearfulness can be symptoms of stress. If you care for a relative or friend and are beginning to suffer from stress of this sort, you should seek help, both for your sake and for the sake of the person you care for.

You could contact Carers UK, which has local groups which can offer emotional support and practical help. Your local Age Concern or social services department should also be able to tell you whether there is a carers' support group in the area. Sharing your problems will probably be a relief in itself.

Contact Carers UK, at the address on page 195, for the address of your nearest group or for advice and support.

In addition, a GP or social worker may be able to organise practical support:

- A home help, home care worker or sitting service may be organised to enable you to get out or have some time to yourself.
- The person you look after may be able to have some day care.
- Respite care may be arranged for a few days or even a week or two to give you a break.

See page 90 for information about holidays for carers.

Invalid Care Allowance (described on page 27) is a social security benefit which gives financial help available to people who look after a severely disabled person for 35 hours a week or more. If you receive Income Support you may qualify for the carer's premium, as explained on page 19.

Age Concern Books' *The Carer's Handbook: What to do and who to turn to* and the other books in the Carers Handbook Series are specially written for anyone who is involved in caring for a relative or friend (details on pages 202–203).

Further information

This final section signposts you to further sources of information. It lists the useful addresses that have been referred to and the other Age Concern publications which may be useful, and ends with an index to help you find your way around the book.

Useful addresses

Age Concern England has a paper titled *Pensioner organisations in England* which describes national organisations run by retired people for themselves and those organisations supporting older people in developing their own activities. If you would like a copy, send a stamped addressed envelope (9in × 6in) to Donna Pearce at Age Concern England at the address on page 197 (quote reference 0702).

CHAPTER 1: MONEY

Association of Investment Trust Companies (AITC)
Durrant House
8–13 Chiswell Street
London EC1Y 4YY
Freephone hotline: 0800 085 8520
Website: www.aitc.co.uk
For a range of factsheets explaining various aspects of investment trusts.

Debt Management Office
Eastcheap Court
11 Philpot Lane
London EC3M 8UD
Tel: 020 7862 6500
Website: www.dmo.gov.uk
Administers gilts for the Government and produces a free guide for private investors.

Department for Work and Pensions (DWP)
Tel: 08457 31 32 33
You can obtain social security leaflets from local social security offices and some post offices. If you have access to the Internet, you can download them (and claim forms for many of the benefits) from the DWP website (www.dwp.gov.uk). Other useful DWP websites are www.info4pensioners.gov.uk and www.pensionguide.gov.uk
The government department responsible for State pensions and social security benefits. It replaced the Department for Social Security (DSS) in 2001. It is now divided into 'Jobcentre Plus', for people of working age, and 'The Pension Service' for all pensions and for benefits for older people.

The Pension Service will have a local service, providing personal contact and working in partnership with other local organisations. This will be supported by 26 'pension centres' which will eventually replace the current service provided by local social security offices. For more information call the number above and ask for the leaflet The Pension Service: a guide to our new service. *For details about your local office, check in the phonebook under 'Jobcentre Plus' or 'social security office', ask at your local library or advice agency or look on the Internet under 'contact us' at www.thepensionservice.gov.uk*

Disability Alliance
Universal House
88–94 Wentworth Street
London E1 7SA
Rights advice line: 020 7247 8763
Website: www.disabilityalliance.org
Provides advice and publications on social security benefits for disabled people.

Financial Ombudsman Service (FOS)
South Quay Plaza
183 Marsh Wall
London E14 9SR
Consumer helpline: 0845 080 1800
Website: www.financial-ombudsman.org.uk
Helps consumers to resolve complaints about most personal finance matters.

Financial Services Authority (FSA)
25 The North Colonnade
Canary Wharf
London E14 5HS
Consumer helpline: 0845 606 1234
Website: www.fsa.gov.uk
An independent body set up by the Government to regulate financial services and protect your rights.

IFA Promotions Ltd
117 Farringdon Road
London EC1R 3BX
Hotline: 0800 085 3250
Website: www.unbiased.co.uk
Can provide a list of IFAs in your area. Also publishes a free booklet on choosing an independent financial adviser.

Inland Revenue
Most Inland Revenue leaflets can be obtained from local tax offices or Inland Revenue Enquiry Centres (look in the phone book under 'Inland Revenue'). Almost all are also available on the website at www.inlandrevenue.gov.uk

Investment Management Association
65 Kingsway
London WC2B 6TD
Hotline: 020 8207 1361
Website: www.investmentfunds.org.uk
For factsheets and a list of all the available unit trusts and OEICs.

MoneyFacts
MoneyFacts House
66–70 Thorpe Road
Norwich NR1 1BJ
Tel: 01603 476476
Website: www.moneyfactsgroup.co.uk
Monthly publication which gives interest rates for all financial institutions. An annual subscription costs £67.50.

Office of the Pensions Advisory Service (OPAS)
11 Belgrave Road
London SW1V 1RB
Tel: 0845 601 2923
Website: www.opas.org.uk
A voluntary organisation which gives advice and information on occupational and personal pensions and helps sort out problems.

The Pension Service
Tyneview Park
Whitley Road
Benton
Newcastle Upon Tyne NE98 1BA
For information about overseas pensions.

Pensions Schemes Registry
PO Box 1NN
Newcastle Upon Tyne NE99 1NN

Tel: 0191 225 6316
Website: www.opra.gov.uk
Helps trace old pension schemes.

Principal Registry of the Family Division
First Avenue House
42–49 High Holborn
London WC1V 6NP
Tel: 020 7947 7000
Website: www.courtservice.gov.uk
Wills can be lodged with the Probate Department, for a charge of £15.

The Public Guardianship Office
Archway Tower
2 Junction Road
London N19 5SZ
Enquiry line: 0845 330 2900 (local call rate)
Enduring Powers of Attorney: 0845 330 2963
Website: www.publictrust.gov.uk
The administrative arm of the Court of Protection.

CHAPTER 2: LEISURE

Age Resource
1268 London Road
London SW16 4ER
Tel: 020 8765 7231
Website: www.ageresource.org.uk
Has a network of 'desks', run by older volunteers, which provide positive ageing information and a venue for computer taster sessions.

Association of British Insurers (ABI)
51 Gresham Street
London EC2V 7HQ
Tel: 020 7600 3333
Website: www.insurance.org.uk
Produces factsheets about different types of insurance.

Association of British Travel Agents (ABTA)
68–71 Newman Street
London W1T 4AH
Tel: 020 7637 2444
Website: www.abta.co.uk
Membership organisation for travel agents and tour operators.

British Executive Service Overseas (BESO)
164 Vauxhall Bridge Road
London SW1V 2RB
Tel: 020 7630 0644
Website: www.beso.org
Charity which sends people on short-term assignments in developing countries.

British Franchise Association (BFA)
Thames View
Newtown Road
Henley-on-Thames
Oxon RG9 1HG
Tel: 01491 578050
Website: www.british-franchise.org
The regulatory body for franchising in the UK.

British Trust for Conservation Volunteers (BTCV)
36 St Mary's Street
Wallingford
Oxon OX10 0EU
Tel: 01491 821600
Website: www.btcv.org.uk
Conservation charity which has groups across the country and which also organises working holidays.

Business Link Network Ltd
Small Business Service
1 Victoria Street
London SW1H 0ET
Tel: 0845 600 9006
Website: www.businesslink.org
Offers support and advice to small businesses.

Camping and Caravanning Club (CCC)

Greenfields House
Westwood Way
Coventry CV4 8JH
Tel: 02476 694995
Website: www.campingandcaravanningclub.co.uk
Membership includes a monthly magazine.

City and Guilds

1 Giltspur Street
London EC1A 9DD
Tel: 020 7294 2850
Website: www.city-and-guilds.co.uk
Publishes a twice-yearly guide to residential short courses for adults.

Community Transport Association (CTA)

Highbank
Halton Street
Hyde
Cheshire SK14 2NY
Tel: 0161 351 1475
For information about community transport groups in your area.

Cyclists' Touring Club (CTC)

69 Meadrow
Godalming
Surrey GU7 3HS
Tel: 0870 873 0060
Website: www.ctc.org.uk
Offers information and technical advice on cycling and cycling holidays.

Department of Transport, Local Government and the Regions; Mobility and Inclusion Unit

Zone 1/11
Great Minster House
76 Marsham Street
London SW1P 4DR
Tel/Textphone: 020 7944 3000
Can provide information about the Blue Badge Parking Scheme.

Hairnet
3 Dean Trench Street
London SW1P 3HB
Tel: 0870 241 5091
Website: www.hairnet.org
Offers computer and internet training and advice to the over 50s.

Holiday Care Service
7th Floor
Sunley House
4 Bedford Park
Croydon
Surrey CRO 2AP
Tel: 0845 124 9971
Website: www.holidaycare.org.uk
National charity which provides specialist information, including over 100 information packs, on holidays for people with special needs. Also maintains a database of respite care facilities in the UK.

Homesitters Ltd
Buckland Wharf
Aylesbury
Bucks HP22 5LQ
Tel: 01296 630730
Website: www.homesitters.co.uk
Arranges homesitting holidays.

Intervac
Coxes Hill Barn
North Wraxall
Chippenham
Wiltshire SN14 7AS
Tel: 01225 892208
Website: www.intervac.co.uk
Long-established home exchange club.

Lion World Travel Ltd
Friendship House
49–51 Gresham Road
Staines

Middlesex TW18 2BF
Tel: 01784 465511
Website: www.friendship-associations.co.uk
Has 'friendship clubs' for people planning reunion holidays.

Mobility Advice and Vehicle Information Service (MAVIS)
Department for Transport
O Wing
MacAdam Avenue
Old Wokingham Road
Crowthorne
Berkshire RG45 6XD
Tel: 01344 661000
Website: www.mobility-unit.dtlr.gov.uk
Offers information and advice to disabled drivers.

Mobility Information Service (MIS)
Unit B1
Greenwood Court
Cartmel Drive
Shrewsbury SY1 2TB
Tel: 01743 463072
Offers information and advice to disabled drivers.

Motability
Goodman House
Station Approach
Harlow
Essex CM20 2ET
Tel: 01279 635666
Website: www.motability.co.uk
Scheme to help disabled people hire or buy cars.

National Adult School Organisation
Riverton
370 Humberstone Road
Leicester LE5 0SA
Tel: 0116 253 8333
Organises local study groups – send an sae for the address of your nearest group.

National Association of Councils for Voluntary Service (NACVS)
Arundel Court
177 Arundel Street
Sheffield S1 2NU
Tel: 0114 278 6636
Website: www.nacvs.org.uk
Contact them to find the address of your local CVS.

National Centre for Volunteering
Regent's Wharf
8 All Saints Street
London N1 9RL
Tel: 020 7520 8900
Website: www.volunteering.org.uk
Produces a range of information on volunteering and runs Volunteers Week annually.

National Extension College (NEC)
The Michael Young Centre
Purbeck Road
Cambridge CB2 2HN
Tel: 01223 400200
Website: www.nec.ac.uk
Offers a free guide to courses.

National Federation of Women's Institutes (NFWI)
104 New King's Road
London SW6 4LY
Tel: 020 7371 9300
Website: www.womens-institute.co.uk
Can give you the address of your local WI.

National Institute of Adult Continuing Education (NIACE)
20 Princess Road West
Leicester LE1 6TP
Tel: 0116 204 4200
Website: www.niace.org.uk
Produces many publications on adult education and organises Adult Learners Week every May.

Open College of the Arts
Registration Department
Freepost SF10678
Barnsley S75 1BR
Freephone: 0800 731 2116
Website: www.oca-uk.com
Charitable trust delivering home-study arts courses.

Open and Distance Learning Quality Council (ODLQC)
16 Park Crescent
London W1B 1AH
Tel: 020 7612 7090
Website: odlqc.org.uk
Independent body which provides information on courses with accredited colleges and general information on distance learning.

Open University
PO Box 724
Milton Keynes MK7 6ZS
Tel: 01908 653231
Website: www.open.ac.uk
The UK's largest university. Offers distance learning courses.

Pre-Retirement Association (PRA)
9 Chesham Road
Guildford
Surrey GU1 3LS
Tel: 01483 301170
Website: www.pra.uk.com
Runs pre-retirement courses and holidays.

RADAR (Royal Association for Disability and Rehabilitation)
12 City Forum
250 City Road
London EC1V 8AF
Tel: 020 7250 3222
Website: www.radar.org.uk
Publishes information on travel and holidays for disabled people.

Ramblers' Association
2nd Floor
Camelford House
87–90 Albert Embankment
London SE1 7TW
Tel: 020 7339 8500
Website: www.ramblers.org.uk
Charity which promotes rambling and protects rights of way. Offers rambling holidays.

REACH
89 Albert Embankment
London SE1 7TP
Tel: 020 7582 6543
Website: www.volwork.org.uk
Matches retired executives with voluntary organisations.

Retired and Senior Volunteer Programme (RSVP)
237 Pentonville Road
London N1 9NJ
Tel: 020 7278 6601
Website: www.csv-rsvp.org.uk
The programme for people over 50 which is part of Community Service Volunteers.

Research Institute for Consumer Affairs (RICA)
30 Angel Gate
City Road
London EC1V 2PT
Tel: 020 7427 2460
Website: www.ricability.org.uk
An independent charity which publishes information on products for older and disabled people.

Saga Holidays Ltd
The Saga Building
Enbrook Park
Folkestone
Kent CT20 3SE
Freephone: 0800 300 500
Website: www.saga.co.uk
Commercial company which runs holidays exclusively for older people.

Single Travellers Action Group (STAG)
Church Lane
Sharnbrook
Bedford MK44 1HR
Send an sae for information about membership (currently £10 a year).
Members receive newsletters giving details of supplement-free hotels and holidays.

Third Age Employment Network (TAEN)
207–221 Pentonville Road
London N1 9UZ
Tel: 020 7843 1590
Website: www.taen.org.uk
Contacts and practical help for those facing age discrimination.

Townswomen's Guild
Chambers of Commerce House
75 Harbourne Road
Edgbaston
Birmingham B15 3DA
Tel: 0121 456 3435
Website: www.townswomen.org.uk
National office which can put you in touch with a local guild.

Tripscope
The Vassall Centre
Gill Avenue
Bristol BS16 2QQ
Helpline: 08457 58 56 41
Website: www.tripscope.org.uk
Transport information service for older and disabled people.

University of the Third Age (U3A)
National Office
26 Harrison Street
London WC1H 8JW
Tel: 020 7837 8838
Website: www.u3a.org.uk
Send a large sae for a list of local U3A groups.

Volunteer Development England
New Oxford House
16 Waterloo Street
Birmingham B2 5UG
Tel: 0121 633 4555
Website: www.vde.org.uk
Contact them to find the address of your local volunteer bureau.

Voluntary Service Overseas (VSO)
317 Putney Bridge Road
London SW15 2PN
Tel: 020 8780 7200
Website: www.vso.org.uk
International development charity that works through volunteers.

Workers' Educational Association (WEA)
17 Victoria Park Square
Bethnal Green
London E2 9PB
Tel: 020 8983 1515
Website: www.wea.org.uk
Organises day and evening classes and weekend residential schools.

CHAPTER 3: HOUSING

The Abbeyfield Society
Abbeyfield House
53 Victoria Street
St Albans
Hertfordshire AL1 3UW
Tel: 01727 857536
Website: www.abbbeyfield.com
For information about Abbeyfield houses across the UK.

AIMS (Advice Information and Mediation Service for retirement housing)
Astral House
1268 London Road
London SW16 4ER

Advice line: 0845 600 2001 (weekdays 9.30am–4.30pm)
Website: www.ageconcern.org.uk/aims
Specialist advice on buying retirement housing.

The Almhouse Association
Billingbear Lodge
Carters Hill
Wokingham
Berkshire RG40 5RU
Tel: 01344 452922
Website: www.almshouses.org
For information on local charities which administer almshouses.

Department for Environment, Food and Rural Affairs (DEFRA) Pet Travel Scheme
PETS Helpline: 0870 241 1710 (weekdays 8.30am–5pm)
PETS website: www.defra.gov.uk/animalh/quarantine
For information about taking pets out of the UK.

EAGA Partnership Ltd
Freepost NEA 12054
Newcastle upon Tyne NE2 1SR
Website: www.eaga.co.uk
Freephone: 0800 316 2808 (weekdays 8am–8pm)
For advice on getting insulation or draughtproofing work done.

Elderly Accommodation Counsel
3rd Floor
89 Albert Embankment
London SE1 7TP
Helpline: 020 7820 1343
Website: www.housingcare.org
Detailed information and advice about all forms of housing for older people. Can provide lists of accommodation to rent or buy in all parts of the UK.

Federation of Master Builders (FMB)
Gordon Fisher House
14–15 Great James Street
London WC1N 3DP
Tel: 020 7242 7583

Website: www.fmb.org.uk
Trade association whose members must adhere to a code of practice.

foundations – the National Co-ordinating Body for Home Improvement Agencies
Bleaklow House
Howard Town Mills
Glossop SK13 8HT
Tel: 01457 891909
Care and Repair Cymru: 029 2057 6286
Care and Repair Forum Scotland: 0141 221 9879
Website: www.foundations.uk.com
Contact foundations to see if there is a care and repair or staying put agency in your area.

Home Improvement Trust
7 Mansfield Road
Nottingham NG1 3FB
Tel: 0115 934 9511
Website: www.hitrust.org
Arranges low cost advances for older people and those with disabilities to make equity release more accessible.

National House Building Council (NHBC)
Buildmark House
Chiltern Avenue
Amersham
Bucks HP6 5AP
Tel: 01494 735363/735369
Website: www.nhbc.co.uk
Has a sheltered housing code of practice.

Office of the Deputy Prime Minister
Free Literature
PO Box 236
Wetherby LS23 7NB
Tel: 0870 1226 236
Website: www.odpm.gov.uk
Produces a number of housing booklets about the rights of tenants.

Ofgem
9 Millbank
London SW1P 3GE
Tel: 020 7901 7000 (Scotland: 0141 331 2678)
Website: www.ofgem.gov.uk
The regulator of the gas and electricity industries. Provides information on changing supplier.

Royal Institute of British Architects (RIBA)
66 Portland Place
London W1B 1AD
Tel: 020 7580 5533
Website: www.architecture.com
Can help you find an architect.

Royal Institution of Chartered Surveyors (RICS)
Surveyor Court
Westwood Way
Coventry CV4 8JE
Tel: 0870 333 1600
Website: www.rics.org.uk
For help in finding a surveyor or information about the Chartered Surveyors Voluntary Service.

CHAPTER 4: HEALTH

Ageing Well
1268 London Road
London SW16 4ER
Tel: 020 8765 7231
Website: www.activage.org.uk
Ageing Well UK has a network of projects aiming to improve and maintain the health of older people. The projects work through older people who are trained as Senior Health Mentors to deliver health messages to other older people.

Arthritis Care
18 Stephenson Way
London NW1 2HD
Freephone Helpline: 0808 800 4050 (weekdays 12pm–4pm)
Website: www.arthritiscare.org.uk
Information and advice and 600 local groups.

Breast Cancer Care
Kiln House
210 New Kings Road
London SW6 4NZ
Helpline: 0808 800 6000 (weekdays 10am–5pm, Saturday 10am–2pm)
Website: www.breastcancercare.org.uk
Information, advice and counselling about breast cancer or other breast-related problems.

British Heart Foundation
14 Fitzhardinge Street
London W1H 6DH
Tel: 020 7935 0185
Publications: 0870 600 6566
Website: www.bhf.org.uk
Publishes a range of booklets on all problems and treatments relating to heart disease.

CancerLink
11–21 Northdown Street
London N1 9BN
Freephone Helpline: 0808 808 2020 (weekdays 9am–6pm)
Website: www.cancerlink.org
Help and support for people with cancer.

Continence Foundation
307 Hatton Square
16 Baldwins Gardens
London EC1N 7RJ
Helpline: 0845 345 0165 (weekdays 9.30am–12.30pm)
Website: www.continence-foundation.org.uk
Information and advice about incontinence.

Diabetes UK
10 Parkway
London NW1 7AA
Careline: 020 7424 1030 (weekdays 9am–5pm)
Website: www.diabetes.org.uk
For advice and support in coping with diabetes.

Drinkline
Freephone: 0800 917 8282
For advice and help if you or someone you know has a drink problem.

Institute of Trichologists
PO Box 142
Stevenage
Hertfordshire SG1 5UX
Write to this address, enclosing an sae, for information about hair and scalp problems.

National Osteoporosis Society (NOS)
Camerton
Bath BA2 0PJ
Helpline: 0845 450 0230
Website: www.nos.org.uk
For information about osteoporosis and a list of specialist centres.

NHS Direct
Tel: 0845 46 47
Website: nhsdirect.nhs.uk
Telephone advice and information service staffed by experienced nurses.

Quitline
Freephone England: 0800 00 22 00
Northern Ireland: 028 9066 3281
Scotland: 0800 84 84 84
Wales: 0345 697 500
For information and help with trying to stop smoking.

Royal National Institute of the Blind (RNIB)
105 Judd Street
London WC1H 9NE
Helpline: 0845 766 9999 (weekdays 9am–5pm)
Website: www.rnib.org.uk
Information to help people with sight problems.

Royal National Institute for Deaf People (RNID)
19–23 Featherstone Street
London EC1Y 8SL
Freephone Helpline: 0808 808 0123

Textphone Helpline: 0808 808 9000
Tinnitus Helpline: 0808 808 6666
Website: www.rnid.org.uk
Information to help people with hearing problems.

Stroke Association
Stroke House
Whitecross Street
London EC1Y 8JJ
Information Service: 0845 3033 100
Website: www.stroke.org.uk
Information and advice about chest, heart and stroke illnesses.

CHAPTER 5: RELATIONSHIPS

Alzheimer's Society
Gordon House
10 Greencoat Place
London SW1P 1PK
Helpline: 0845 300 0336
Website: www.alzheimers.org.uk
For people with Alzheimer's Disease, and other forms of dementia, and their families and carers.

British Association for Sexual and Marital Therapy
PO Box 13686
London SW20 9ZH
Tel: 020 8543 2707
Website: www.basrt.org.uk
Send an sae for information about the availability of therapy for sexual difficulties.

British Humanist Association
47 Theobalds Road
London WC1X 8SP
Tel: 020 7430 0908
Website: www.humanism.org.uk
For information about non-religious funerals.

Carers UK

20–25 Glasshouse Yard
London EC1A 4JT
Helpline: 0808 808 7777 (weekdays 10am–12pm and 2pm–4pm)
Website: www.carersonline.org.uk
Provides help and advice for all carers.

Crossroads Association

10 Regent Place
Rugby CV21 2PN
Tel: 01788 573653
Website: www.crossroads.org.uk
Contact them to find out if there is a scheme to relieve carers in the area.

Cruse – Bereavement Care

126 Sheen Road
Richmond
Surrey TW9 1UR
Helpline: 0870 167 1677
Website: www.crusebereavementcare.org.uk
Offers bereavement counselling and a range of publications.

Disabled Living Foundation (DLF)

380–384 Harrow Road
London W9 2HU
Helpline: 0845 130 9177 (weekdays 10am–4pm)
Website: www.dlf.org.uk
Provides specialist advice and information on disability equipment and adaptations.

National Association of Funeral Directors (NAFD)

618 Warwick Road
Solihull
West Midlands B91 1AA
Tel: 0121 711 1343
Website: www.nafd.org.uk
Independent trade association with its own code of practice.

Relate
Herbert Gray College
Little Church Street
Rugby
Warwickshire CV21 3AP
Tel: 0845 456 1310
Website: www.relate.org.uk
Can provide the address of your local branch for counselling for difficult relationships.

SPOD (The Association to Aid the Sexual and Personal Relationships of People with a Disability)
286 Camden Road
London N7 0BJ
Tel: 020 7607 8851
Helpline: 020 7607 9191 (Tuesdays and Thursdays, 11am–2pm)
Provides an advisory and counselling service for people with disabilities.

Womens Royal Voluntary Service (WRVS)
Milton Hill House
Milton Hill
Abingdon
Oxon OX13 6AD
Tel: 01235 442900
Website: www.wrvs.org.uk
Runs a nationwide network of community services, using volunteers (including men).

About Age Concern

Your Guide to Retirement is one of a wide range of publications produced by Age Concern England, the National Council on Ageing. Age Concern works on behalf of all older people and believes later life should be fulfilling and enjoyable. For too many this is impossible. As the leading charitable movement in the UK concerned with ageing and older people, Age Concern finds effective ways to change that situation.

Where possible, we enable older people to solve problems themselves, providing as much or as little support as they need. A network of local Age Concerns, supported by many thousands of volunteers, provides community-based services such as lunch clubs, day centres and home visiting.

Nationally, we take a lead role in campaigning, parliamentary work, policy analysis, research, specialist information and advice provision, and publishing. Innovative programmes promote healthier lifestyles and provide older people with opportunities to give the experience of a lifetime back to their communities.

Age Concern is dependent on donations, covenants and legacies.

Age Concern England
1268 London Road
London SW16 4ER
Tel: 020 8765 7200
Fax: 020 8765 7211

Age Concern Cymru
4th Floor
1 Cathedral Road
Cardiff CF11 9SD
Tel: 029 2037 1566
Fax: 029 2039 9562

Age Concern Scotland
113 Rose Street
Edinburgh EH2 3DT
Tel: 0131 220 3345
Fax: 0131 220 2779

Age Concern Northern Ireland
3 Lower Crescent
Belfast BT7 1NR
Tel: 028 9024 5729
Fax: 028 9023 5497

Publications from Age Concern Books

Your Rights: A guide to money benefits for older people

Sally West

A highly acclaimed annual guide to the State benefits available to older people. Contains current information on Jobseeker's Allowance, Incapacity Benefit, Income Support, Housing Benefit and Retirement Pensions, among other matters, and includes advice on how to claim them.

£4.99   0-86242-363-5

Your Taxes and Savings: A guide for older people

Paul Lewis

Explains how the tax system affects older people over retirement age, including how to avoid paying more than necessary. The information about savings and investments is updated annually and covers the wide range of opportunities now available.

£5.99   0-86242-365-1

The Pensions Handbook: Planning ahead to boost retirement income

Sue Ward

Explores in detail the main types of pension scheme – state, occupational, personal and stakeholder – and offers guidance on increasing their value. Specific topics examined include: changing jobs; returning to work after a break; stakeholder pensions; pension issues for women; different types of pension annuity; the new Second State Pension (S2P); and pension safety.

Clearly written in jargon-free language, this completely revised and updated guide is an important stepping-stone towards better financial security in retirement.

£6.99   0-86242-378-3

Using Your Home as Capital

Cecil Hinton and David McGrath

This best-selling book for home owners, which is updated annually, gives a detailed explanation of how to capitalise on the value of your home and obtain a regular additional income.

£4.99   0-86242-377-5

Changing Direction: Employment options in mid-life: 2nd edition

Sue Ward

The new edition of this topical and higly practical book is designed to help those aged 40–55 get back to work. It helps readers understand their own skills, shows how to look for a job and guides readers through the many positive steps which can be taken. It looks at issues such as:

- adjusting to change
- opportunities for work
- working for yourself
- retraining and education
- age discrimination
- finances.

Complete with a range of personal accounts, this book is a first point of reference for those in mid-life to take control of their working lives again.

£9.99   0-86242-331-7

Getting the Most from your Computer

Jackie Sherman

This book ranges from the basics of buying and setting up a system, through an introduction to all the commonly-used packages such as Word, Excel and PowerPoint, to more advanced topics so that readers can learn how to create a website, produce animated presentations, run their own budget on a spreadsheet or use the desktop publishing features of a word processing package.

£5.99   0-86242-346-5

How to be a Silver Surfer: A beginner's guide to the internet for the over 50s

Emma Aldridge

This book is a companion guide for people who are new to the Internet and a little apprehensive about what to do. Using simple step-by-step explanations, it helps readers through the most important tasks when first using the Internet. Topics include searching the Web, sending an email and saving a favourite Web page for future reference.

£4.99   0-86242-336-8

A Buyer's Guide to Retirement Housing: Revised edition 2001

Co-published with ROOM (National Council for Housing and Planning)

This book is designed to answer many of the questions older people may have when looking to buy a flat or bungalow in a sheltered scheme. It provides comprehensive information for retired people, and their families and friends, including topics such as: housing options; the design and management of schemes; making the purchase; arrangements for reselling and other important rights. Detailed advice is also provided on areas such as the running costs, location and terms of ownership. This popular book – now in its third edition – will provide all the information needed to make an informed decision.

£6.99   0-86242-339-2

Alive and Kicking

Julie Sobczak

Activity can play a major part in helping older people to remain agile and independent. Regular exercise can optimise levels of fitness required for the daily tasks of living, encourage social contacts, improve the feeling of well-being and help prevent future health problems. With the wealth of ideas contained in this book, health professionals, day centre managers, care home managers, activity organisers, relatives and carers will find plenty to stimulate the imagination.

£11.99   0-86242-289-2

Healthy Eating on a Budget

Sara Lewis

This book shows how, even on a tight budget, it is possible to produce meals that are both healthy and delicious. There are 100-plus closely costed recipes for the health-conscious cook, all of which are flagged up to show their nutritional values and calorie content.

£6.95   0-86242-170-5

Eating Well on a Budget

Sara Lewis

This book offers sound advice on shopping and cooking cost-effectively and includes wholesome original recipes for four complete weekly menus.

£2.50   0-86242-120-9

Better Health in Retirement

Dr Anne Roberts

Topics covered include:

- developing a healthy lifestyle
- common illnesses in later life
- help for older carers

- health checks and screening
- using the health service

£6.99   0-86242-251-5

Know your Complementary Therapies

Eileen Inge Herzberg

People who practise natural medicine all share a common basic belief: that we can all heal ourselves – we just need a little help from time to time. Uniquely focusing on complementary therapies and older people, the book covers acupuncture, herbal medicine, aromatherapy, spiritual healing, homeopathy and osteopathy. It helps readers to decide which therapies are best suited to their needs, and where to go for help.

£9.99   0-86242-309-0

The Carers Handbook Series

The Carers Handbook series has been written for the carers, families and friends of older people. It guides readers through key care situations and aims to help them make informed, practical decisions. All the books in the series:

- offer step-by-step guidance on decisions which need to be taken
- examine all the options available
- include practical checklists and case studies
- point you towards specialist help
- guide you through the social services maze
- are up to date with recent guidelines and issues
- draw on Age Concern's wealth of experience.

Caring for someone with a sight problem

Marina Lewycka £6.99 0-86242-381-3

Caring for someone with cancer

Toni Battison £6.99 0-86242-382-1

Caring for someone with arthritis

Jim Pollard £6.99 0-86242-373-2

Caring for someone with diabetes

Marina Lewycka £6.99 0-86242-374-0

Caring for someone with a heart problem

Toni Battison £6.99 0-86242-371-6

Caring for someone at a distance

Julie Spencer-Cingöz £6.99 0-86242-367-8

Caring for someone with an alcohol problem

Mike Ward £6.99 0-86242-372-4

The Carer's Handbook: What to do and who to turn to

Marina Lewycka   £6.99   0-86242-366-X

Finding and paying for residential and nursing home care

Marina Lewycka   £6.99   0-86242-376-7

Caring for someone who is dying

Penny Mares   £6.99   0-86242-370-8

Caring for someone who has dementia

Jane Brotchie   £6.99   0-86242-368-6

Caring for someone who has had a stroke

Philip Coyne & Penny Mares

£6.99   0-86242-369-4

Choices for the carer of an elderly relative

Marina Lewycka   £6.99   0-86242-375-9

Caring for someone with a hearing loss

Marina Lewycka   £6.99   0-86242-380-5

If you would like to order any of these titles, please write to the address below, enclosing a cheque or money order for the appropriate amount, plus £1.95 post and packing, made payable to Age Concern England. Credit card orders may be made on 0870 44 22 044 (individuals) or 0870 44 22 120 (AC federation, other organisations and institutions). Fax: 0870 44 22 034.

Age Concern Books
PO Box 232
Newton Abbot
Devon TQ12 4XQ

Age Concern Information Line/Factsheets subscription

Age Concern produces more than 45 comprehensive factsheets designed to answer many of the questions older people (or those advising them) may have. Subjects covered include money and benefits, health, community care, leisure and education, and housing. For up to five free factsheets, telephone: 0800 00 99 66 (7am-7pm, seven days a week, every day of the year). Alternatively you may prefer to write to Age Concern, FREEPOST (SWB 30375), ASHBURTON, Devon TQ13 7ZZ.

For professionals working with older people, the factsheets are available on an annual subscription service, which includes updates throughout the year. For further details and costs of the subscription, please write to Age Concern at the above Freepost address.

Index

Abbeyfield houses 102
abroad, going 103–106
   medical treatment 87
   receiving pensions 8
   taking pets 105
   voluntary work 85
   see also holidays
access guides 80
activity holidays 81–82
adaptations (to the home) 113–14, 168
Age Concern 56, 59–60, 61, 67, 82, 89, 197
   publications 198–204
Age Resource 55, 56, 62
ageism 68–69
agents 49
aids and equipment 168–169
AIMS 97
air travel 75, 78
alarm systems 108–109
alcohol consumption 129
almshouses 102
annuities
   pension fund 15–17
   purchased life 43–44
appointees 51
arthritis 137–138, 153
Attendance Allowance 26, 27, 167, 172
attorneys, appointing 50–51

banks and building societies 37
   accounts 32, 37–38
   executorship accounts 164
   opening joint accounts 49
   share-dealing services 41
   using another person's account 52
benefits and allowances
   for carers 27
   collecting for another person 49, 51, 52
   and holidays abroad 88
   for people with disabilities 24–26
   for people with low incomes 17–23
bereavement 157–159
bereavement counsellors 62, 159
blood pressure, high 128, 132, 142–143
Blue Badge Scheme 80
bonds 39, 41, 44
British Trust for Conservation Volunteers 60, 81
builders, finding 112
building societies see banks and building societies
buses 74, 76
Business Link 65, 70–71
businesses 70–71
   buying existing 71
   buying franchises 72
   starting from scratch 72

calluses 136
camping 83, 85–86
cancer 138–139
Canvas Holidays 86
Capital Gains Tax 29, 32–33
car driving 79–80, 88
caravanning 83, 85–86
Care and Repair 110
carers
   benefits 27
   community services 169–171
   holidays 90
   social services assessments 169
   support for 169, 170, 173–174
   when person lives with you 166–167
Carer's Allowance 27
casual work 66–67
central heating systems 117
chimneys, inspecting 111
chiropody 136, 147, 171
cholesterol 127, 129
clubs, joining 59–60, 156

coach travel 75, 76, 77
Cold Weather payments 23
community care services 169–171
community involvement 59–60
community minibuses 76
computers 55
condensation 116
consultancies 71
corns 136
corporate bonds 41
Cosmos: 'Golden Times' holidays 82
council housing 94–95, 99
   buying 95, 97, 100
   for disabled people 103
   exchanges 99–100
   extra-care 103
Council Tax Benefit 10, 17, 21–22
Council Tax reductions 22
Court of Protection 51, 52
   credits 4, 9
Cruse Bereavement Care 159
CVs 69
cycling 81, 82, 83, 126

dancing 126
day care 170
deafness 141–142
death
   arrangements to be made 47–48,
      161–162
   and bereavement 157–159
   registering 159–160
   see also probate, dealing with; wills
degrees, taking 58
dental care 133–135, 147
dentures, care of 134
depression 154, 157, 158
diabetes 132, 140, 141
dial-a-rides 78
diet 127–130, 140, 145
dieting 132
disabilities, people with
   aids and adaptations 113–114,
      168–169
   benefits 24–26

holidays 89–90
housing 103; *see also* retirement
   housing
   transport and travel 76–80
Disability Living Allowance 25–26, 172
disabled facilities grants 113–114
district nurses 171
divorced people
   and pensions 5, 12–13
   and wills 46–47
doors 107, 111, 112, 114, 115, 116
draughtproofing 114–116
driving 79–80, 88
driving licences 79

E coli 131
earning *see* work
eating *see* diet
education *see* learning opportunities
electrical wiring, inspecting 111
electricity suppliers 117
employment *see* work
employment agencies 67–68, 69
Employment Credit 67
Enduring Powers of Attorney (EPAs)
   50–51, 52
environmental groups 60
equipment 168–169
equity release schemes 118–121
Eurocamp 86
exercise 124–127, 132, 143, 145
Experience Corps 63
eye problems 141
eye tests 141, 147

fat, dietary 127–28
ferries 76, 78
fibre, dietary 129
financial matters
   advice on 35–36
   managing another person's money
      49–52
   see also benefits; grants; pensions;
      savings and investments
Financial Services Authority 16, 35, 120

floors, inspecting 111–112
fluid intake 129
food poisoning 130–131
foot care 135–136, 140
franchises, buying 72
freeholds, buying 100–101
Friends of the Earth 60, 61
fuel bills, help with 23, 117
funeral arrangements 47, 161–162

galleries, visiting 54
gas suppliers 117
government stock/'gilt-edged
    securities'/'gilts' 33, 39–40
Graduated Pensions 7
grants
    disabilities facilities 113–114
    for fuel 23
    holidays 89
    insulation and draughtproofing 116
    repairs and improvements 23, 112–113
    training 65, 67
gum disease 133
guttering, inspecting 111

hair loss 136
Hairnet 55
health
    and exercise 124–127
    problems 137–146
health care
    abroad 87
    help with costs 24, 147–148
hearing problems 141–142
heart disease 127, 130, 132, 142, 153
heating 117
Holiday Care Service 89, 90
holidays 81–83
    affording 89
    for carers 90
    long-stay 83–86
    for people with disabilities 89–90
    planning 86–88
    for single people 83
    see also travel and transport

home care assistants/home helps 170,
    174
Home Energy Efficiency Scheme see
    Warm Front Grants
home improvements see repairs and
    improvements
home income plans 119
Home Responsibilities Protection 4
home reversion schemes 118, 120
home swapping 84–85, 89, 100
homes, care 171–173
HOMES Mobility Scheme 100
homesitting 89
homosexuality 156
Hormone Replacement Therapy
    145–146
hot water cylinder jackets 115
houses
    buying abroad 103–104, 105–106
    buying freehold 100–101
    heating 117
    and moving 92–93
    raising income or capital from
        118–21
    renting see rented accommodation
    security 88, 107, 108–109
    ventilating 116
    see also repairs and improvements;
        retirement housing
housing associations 94, 95, 97, 99
    exchanges 99–100
    extra-care housing 103
    housing for disabled people 103
    and right to buy 100
    Tenants' Incentive Scheme 100
Housing Benefit 10, 17, 21–22
HRT see Hormone Replacement Therapy

immunisation 87
impotence 154
Incapacity Benefit 3, 9, 10, 24–25
Income Bonds 39
Income Support 10, 18–20, 147, 167
Income Tax 28–32
    and self-employment 73

incontinence 143–144, 153, 170
Inheritance Tax 33–34, 164
insulation 114–116
insurance
    car 79–80, 88
    holiday 87
Internet, the 55, 66
interviews, preparing for 70
intestacy 46
Invalid Care Allowance 4, 27, 174
investment bonds 44
investment trusts 42–43
investments *see* savings and investments
ISAs (Individual Savings Accounts) 38,
    42, 43

job advertisements 68
Jobcentres/Jobcentre Plus offices 66, 67
Jobseeker's Allowance 4, 9–10, 147
job-sharing 66

keep-fit classes 126

laundry services 170
Learndirect 56, 65
learning opportunities
    'distance' 57–58
    informal 54–55
    local adult education classes 55–56
    residential courses 57
    taking degrees 58
Leasehold Schemes for the Elderly 97, 98
legal fees, help with 24
libraries 54, 62
Lion World Travel 82
listeria 131
loans
    interest-only 114, 119
    and legal protection 120–121
    ordinary 119
    roll-up 118–119, 120
loft insulation 115

marriage: and wills 46
marriage bureaux 156
Married Couple's Allowance 31, 32

married women's pensions 5, 9
masturbation 155
MAVIS 79
meals-on-wheels 170
mentally incapable people
    managing financial affairs for 51–52
    and powers of attorney 50–51
minerals 129
Minimum Income Guarantee *see* Income
    Support
mobility aids 168
Mobility Information Service (MIS) 79
mortgages, interest-only 98
Motability scheme 26, 79
moving house 92–93
    see also abroad, going; retirement
    housing
museums, visiting 54

National Adult School Organisation 56
National Express 75, 76
National Extension College 57–58
National Savings 33, 35, 38–39
National Trust 61
National Vocational Qualifications 65
'networking' 68
New Deal 50 Plus 67
nursing care 169
nursing homes *see* homes, care

occupational pensions 6, 11–14
occupational therapists (OTs) 168–169
Open College of the Arts 57
Open-ended Investment Companies 43
Open University 57, 58
Orange Badge Scheme *see* Blue Badge
    Scheme
osteoporosis 145–146

package holidays 84
parking concessions 80
part-time work 66
passports 86–87
pelvic muscle exercises 143–144
Pension Credit 17, 20–21
pension forecasts 4

pensioner bonds 39
pensions
    collecting for another person 49, 51,
        52
    occupational 6, 11–14
    personal 6, 14–17, 32
    State 2–11, 30
pesticides 131
pilates 126
plumbing, inspecting 111
post-mortem examinations 160
powers of attorney 50–51
Premium Bonds 39
Pre-Retirement Association 56
prescriptions 147
probate, dealing with 162–165
Public Guardianship Office 52
purchased life annuities 43–44

RADAR 80, 90
radio
    learning opportunities 54
    job advertisements 68
railcards 74–75
Ramblers' Association 60, 82
REACH 63
Relate 61, 62, 154
relationships
    finding new partners 155–156
    and sexual problems 154
rented accommodation 98–99, 100
    abroad 104
    see also council tenants; retirement
        housing
repairs and improvements 110–112
    aids and adaptations 113–114,
        168–169
    finding builders 112
    grants for 23, 112–114
    insulation and draughtproofing
        114–116
residential homes see homes, care
respite care 170, 174
Retired and Senior Volunteer Programme
    63

retirement housing 93–95, 101
    Abbeyfield houses 102
    almshouses 102
    buying 94, 95–97
    for disabled people 103
    extra-care 103
    Leasehold Schemes for the Elderly 97,
        98
    for people with limited capital 97–98
    renting 94, 95
    shared ownership schemes 97, 98
reunion holidays 82
roll-up loans 118–119, 120
roofs, inspecting 111, 112
Rover tickets 76
Royal Society for the Protection of Birds
    60

Safe Home Income Plans campaign 120
Saga Holidays 82
salmonella 130–131
salt 128, 143
Samaritans 61, 62
savings and investments 35
    advice on 35–37
    bank and building accounts 32,
        37–38
    corporate bonds 41
    government stock 39–40
    indirect investments 42–44
    National Savings 38–39
    shares 41
    and tax 30, 32
sea travel 76, 78
security, home 88, 107, 108–109
self-employment 70–72
    and pensions 15
    and tax 73
sensate focusing 152
SERPS (State Earnings-Related Pension
    Scheme) 6, 12
sexual relations 150
    improving 151–153
    problems 153–155
shares 41

sheltered housing *see* retirement housing
SHIP *see* Safe Home Income Plan
   campaign
sight tests 141, 147
sitting schemes 170
smoking 132–133, 143
social cars 78
Social Fund 17, 22–23, 108, 114
social services' assessments 169–170
societies, joining 59–60, 156
solicitors, finding 46
spectacles 147
stakeholder pensions 14–15
Stamp Duty 93
State Second Pension (S2P) 6, 7, 12
Staying Put 110
stress 143, 173
stress incontinence 143–144
strokes 132, 142, 143, 153
S2P *see* State Second Pension
sugar 128
swimming 125–126

Tai-chi 126
taxes *see* Capital Gains Tax; Income Tax;
   Inheritance Tax
taxicard schemes 78
teeth, care of 133–135
telephones 108
television programmes, learning from 54
teleworking 67
temporary work 66–67
tenancies *see* rented accommodation
Third Age Employment Network 69
'third party mandates' 49
toenails, cutting 135, 171
town twinning holidays 81
Townswomen's Guild 60
training, further 65
   grants 67
trains 74–75, 77
travel and transport
   air 75, 78
   buses 74, 76
   coaches 75, 76, 77

concessionary 24, 74–76
   door-to-door transport 78
   for fun 76
   hospital travel costs 147
   for people with disabilities 76–80
   by sea 76, 78
   trains 74–75, 77
   see also car driving; holidays
Tripscope 80

unit trusts 42
universities 58
University of the Third Age 56

vaginal dryness 154
ventilation 116
Viagra 154
visas 86–87
vitamins 129
voluntary work 60, 61–63, 78
   abroad 85

walking 60, 82, 83, 125
walls, inspecting 111
Warm Front Grants 116
water consumption 129
weight, losing 132, 143
widowers' pensions 5–6, 7
widows' pensions 5, 6, 7
wills 45–47, 159
   see also probate, dealing with
windows 107, 111, 114, 115, 116
Winter Fuel Payments 23
wiring, inspecting 111
Women's Institute 60
work 64–65
   advice on 66
   and ageism 68–69
   for an employer 66–70
   and retirement pensions 8
   see also self-employment; voluntary
      work
Workers' Educational Association 56
working holidays 81

yoga 126